Dinner on Hand

Kraft Kitchens

Dinner on Hand

Easy everyday recipes you can make tonight

Random House Canada

National Library of Canada Cataloguing in Publication
Main entry under title:
Dinner on Hand: Easy everyday recipes you can make tonight / The Kraft Kitchens.
Includes index.
ISBN 0-679-31218-8

1. Quick and easy cookery. I. Kraft Kitchens.
TX833.5.D45 2002 641.5'55 C2002-901641-X

10 9 8 7 6 5 4 3 2 1

Text and cover design by: Vicki Hornsby
Cover photography by: Michael Kohn
Printed and bound in the United States of America
www.randomhouse.ca

Cover: Mix-and-Match Chicken Bake, page 66

The following brands are a part of the Kraft family of tasty and convenient products. In many of the recipes in this book, you'll find shortened references to them. Their full names are given here to help you when you shop:

BAKER'S Unsweetened Baking Chocolate

CHEEZ WHIZ Cheese Dip

CHEEZ WHIZ Cheese Dip with Jalapeño Peppers

COOL WHIP Whipped Topping

CRYSTAL LIGHT Lemonade Flavor Low Calorie
Soft Drink Mix

CRYSTAL LIGHT Tangerine Grapefruit Flavor
Low Calorie Soft Drink Mix

HONEY MAID Honey Grahams

JELL-O Gelatin

JELL-O Instant Pudding & Pie Filling

JELL-O Pudding Snacks

JELL-O Vanilla Flavor Instant Pudding
& Pie Filling

KOOL-AID Unsweetened Soft Drink Mix

KRAFT Barbecue Sauce

KRAFT CATALINA Dressing

KRAFT Dressing

KRAFT 100% Grated Parmesan Cheese

KRAFT Macaroni & Cheese Dinner

KRAFT MAYO Real Mayonnaise

KRAFT Mexican Style Shredded Cheese

KRAFT Shredded Cheese

KRAFT Singles

MINUTE White Rice

MIRACLE WHIP Salad Dressing

OREO Chocolate Sandwich Cookies

PHILADELPHIA Cream Cheese Spread

PHILADELPHIA Chive & Onion Cream
Cheese Spread

POST SPOON SIZE Shredded Wheat

RITZ Crackers

SHAKE 'N BAKE Seasoned Coating Mix

STOVE TOP Stuffing Mix

TRISCUIT Crackers

VELVEETA Pasteurized Prepared
Cheese Product

WHEAT THINS Snack Crackers

Contents

INTRODUCTION 1

SNACKS & STARTERS 11

MAIN DISHES 29
    9 x 13s: The Best Baked Casseroles 31
    One-Skillet Stovetop Solutions 44
    Meat – and Fish – Mainly 58
    Everyday Favorites from around the World 75
    Sandwiches and Burgers 95
    Dinnertime Options with a Personal Touch 111
    Main-Dish Vegetables and Greens 120

SIDES & SALADS 133

DESSERTS 163

At the Kraft Kitchens

Here are the people who helped bring you the book you are holding right now:

Recipe Content Team
Cécile Girard-Hicks, Stephanie Williams, Lorna Roberts, Tracy Sherva, Susanne Stark, Michele McAdoo

Recipe Development
Karen Didier, Lisa Brandt-Whittington, Marla Goldberg, Maxine Karpel, Kathleen Mackintosh, Cayla Runka

Recipe Editors
Betty Heinlen, Heather Melrose

Marketing Team
Maureen Weiss, Carol Blindauer, Gillian Fripp, Irene Huang, Jill Nykoliation

Photography
All photography produced by Michael Kohn, photographer; Sue Henderson, food stylist; Catherine MacFadyen, prop stylist; Vicki Hornsby, art director; Ashley Denton, food-styling assistant; Shelagh McAuliffe, photography assistant; except for that which appears on pages 34, 88 and 117 (Gibson & Smith Photography); 42 (Jurek Wyszynski); and 43, 80 and 81 (Shun Sasabuchi).

To everyone who has reached out to us with thoughtful comments, hard questions and personal insights about their families and food and everyday living, a sincere thank-you – from all of us at the Kraft Kitchens.

By mail, on our toll-free phone lines, at our cooking schools and through our websites, you're the ones who keep us grounded in real home cooking. We are constantly learning from the many experiences you share with us and we're honored to be a part of your life.

Introduction
MAKING FAMILY FOOD SIMPLE

At the Kraft Kitchens our goal is to make family food simpler, quicker and more delicious than you ever thought it could be. We work to improve on familiar recipes and develop simpler ways of doing things. To anyone who has ever wished it was easier to put family-pleasing dinners on the table, we say, "This is just what you've been looking for!"

When we look at a recipe here in the Kraft Kitchens, we start by asking how we can take the dish down to its essentials, cutting out all the extra steps that just don't need to be there. We think about what's at the heart of the dish, the basic good taste that's there when you've lifted away the complicated methods and the technical vocabulary. And that's what we want to share with you.

Cooking this way means everyday language, common skills and learning to build on the mental cookbook that you, the home cook, have inside. What's a mental cookbook? It's simple, really.

Just ask yourself how many dinnertime dishes you know by heart. If you're like most home cooks, your mental-cookbook list will have somewhere between 5 and 15 different dishes on it, easy family favorites that taste great and always turn out right. You grab a skillet, pull a few ingredients off the shelf and before you know it dinner's on the table and everyone's happy.

With *Dinner on Hand*, you're about to discover that your mental cookbook has just expanded to include hundreds of new dinner ideas. Because we've tested every recipe in this book with different equipment, in different ovens, even with different people doing the cooking, we know they're going to work for you.

WHAT THIS MEANS FOR YOU IS:
- A few quick and easy steps
- Familiar on-hand ingredients
- Cleanup that's done before you know it

MAKING YOUR EVERYDAY COOKING EASIER

**HOW WE DEMYSTIFY
EVERYDAY COOKING**

It's easiest for us to explain
the process by comparing
the method we once used
to explain a recipe (we'll
use a stir-fry here) with
the way we approach the
same dish today.

Twenty years ago, our method of putting together a chicken stir-fry was
a traditional one that looked pretty much like this:

CHICKEN STIR-FRY

4 medium-sized boneless chicken breasts, cut into strips	1/4 tsp ground ginger
2 tbsp oil	2-1/2 cups bean sprouts
1 cup celery, thinly sliced	1 can water chestnuts, drained and sliced
1 medium green pepper, cut into strips	1/2 cup chicken broth
1 small onion, sliced	2 tbsp soy sauce
1 tsp salt	2 tbsp cornstarch

Add chicken to hot oil in a large skillet and stir-fry for 2 to 3 minutes. Add celery,
green pepper, onion, salt and ginger; stir-fry until vegetables are tender-crisp. Add
bean sprouts, water chestnuts and chicken broth. Combine soy sauce and cornstarch;
mix until smooth. Gradually stir soy mixture into chicken-broth mixture and cook,
stirring constantly, until sauce is thickened. Serve over prepared rice. Serves 4.

When we thought about it, that traditional stir-fry seemed like a lot of work.
It was, after all, just some meat, vegetables and sauce, served over rice.

So we began to undo the process, replacing 5 separate measured ingredients (and the inescapable challenge of keeping the cornstarch from
lumping) with a splash of flavorful salad dressing as the foundation of
our sauce. A few minor ingredients – like those water chestnuts – got lost
along the way and we focused on the easy-to-grasp rules of thumb that would

always work: a pound of meat for 4 people and a handful of each of the vegetables per person. We'd leave it up to you to cover a pan or leave it uncovered (although if it was important to do one or the other, we'd be sure to tell you).

And suddenly our stir-fry wasn't so complicated. In fact, with that stir-fry we were able to take the whole process down to 3 simple steps: starting the meat on its own; adding vegetables to the skillet partway through; then finishing the dish with some dressing to make the sauce.

Here's the result. With our recipes we utilize easy-to-follow 4-color grids – which show 4 tasty combinations of popular meat, vegetables and flavorings – to get you started. After you've practiced our approach it really becomes exciting, as you use the same simple process to mix and match ingredients to perfectly satisfy your own family's tastes.

THE SIMPLE STIR-FRY

Just follow our 3 simple steps:

1 STIR-FRY sliced **meat** (1 lb should do it for 4) with a bit of Kraft **dressing** for 10 minutes.

2 ADD sliced **veggies** (a handful per person) and cook 10 minutes more.

3 STIR in an additional 1/2 cup dressing to make a sauce. Serve over prepared rice.

And use the ingredients you have on hand …

What **meat** do you feel like?	What **veggies** are on hand?	Add a **dressing**
chicken breast	cauliflower, peppers, broccoli	sun-dried tomato
beef sirloin	celery, carrots	Italian
pork loin	red cabbage, apples, onions	Catalina
meatless	carrots, broccoli, onions, cauliflower	Italian

THE DINNER-ON-HAND PANTRY

WE KNOW WHAT
EVERYDAY COOKS
HAVE ON HAND:

- Ground beef and chicken
- Cheese, milk, butter and eggs
- Fruits and vegetables
- Familiar spices
- Bread, rice and potatoes

The thing about a pantry – at least as we define it – is that it's made up of useful, versatile staples and perishables that are there already in your house. We start with the same foods you shop for every week: meat and dairy, fruits and vegetables, bread and other starches. We pay attention to what you've told us about what you have on hand and what your family likes to eat. When you look at the recipes in *Dinner on Hand*, you're going to find you can reach into your cupboards or open your refrigerator and just start cooking. No special shopping trip required.

At left are the foods we know everyday cooks have on hand. Sound familiar? They're what we have in our kitchens, too. We use branded products that are trusted family favorites in our testing. So, when we share a recipe that works well for us, we know we can guarantee the same good results in your kitchen.

FAST, FASTER, FASTEST

In the process of rethinking our whole approach to everyday cooking, we took a good look at the vegetables we used all the time. We realized that one of the most useful ways to categorize them in our mental cookbooks was in terms of the cooking time they required. Our Fast, Faster, Fastest approach here breaks things down into 2-minute, 5-minute and 10-minute vegetable groupings. Now we automatically know how to organize our preparations, getting the 10-minute vegetables ready to go first, then chopping the others that require less cooking in order of the time they need to cook.

FAST:
10-MINUTE VEGETABLES

Onions, potatoes, carrots, broccoli, cauliflower, eggplant, sweet potatoes, leeks, beets, parsnips, turnips and portobello mushrooms

FASTER:
5-MINUTE VEGETABLES

Peppers, green beans, tomatoes, asparagus, celery and shredded cabbage

FASTEST:
2-MINUTE VEGETABLES

Spinach, zucchini, button mushrooms, kernel corn, peas, snow peas and bean sprouts

EQUIPPING THE DINNER-ON-HAND KITCHEN

In our work, as at home, the Kraft Kitchens like to keep it simple. The fewer pots, gadgets and appliances we depend on, the less there is to organize or clean.

KNIVES

For most purposes all you need are a chef's knife, a bread knife and a paring knife, with a butcher's steel to keep them sharp. Of these, the chef's knife is the most versatile: The blade is usually between 6 and 8 inches in length and it's just the right size, if your knife is a good one, to make cutting and chopping a breeze. A long, thin serrated bread knife is the one you want for breads and cakes – and also for fresh tomatoes. A paring knife, small, flexible and the most inexpensive of the three, is essential for preparing small fruits and vegetables. A carving knife may have some appeal, if you cook a lot of roasts, but in most cases a chef's knife will do the same job quite well.

POTS AND PANS

Where pots and pans are concerned, we fall back once more on the rule of 3. Our basics are a 9- x 13-inch baking dish (the workhorse of our kitchen, for roasts, casseroles and other baking); a large saucepan (for fast one-pot suppers, pasta, rice, potatoes and vegetables); and a large nonstick skillet (for stir-fries, egg dishes and pasta sauces). These, plus our trusty broiler pan, are what we use to get dinner on the table.

CUTTING BOARDS

Consider having a plastic cutting board for meats (you can sanitize it in the dishwasher after every use) and a wooden board (which you should hand wash in order to prolong its working life) for vegetables and breads. Place a damp cloth underneath boards when you use them, to prevent them from slipping on you.

APPLIANCES

Kitchen appliances are a mixed blessing: Even though they can reduce time and effort, they add another element to kitchen cleanup. We try to keep the use of them to a minimum and in our recipes for you we also suggest alternative methods. Our favorite kitchen appliance is surely the microwave oven and we use it frequently to help speed things along. When we use other kitchen equipment, we make it a practice to use what you would use at home.

UTENSILS

We like big long-handled spoons, plastic, wood and metal, and we keep a whisk for smoothing out sauces. A metal strainer/colander is also useful.

Out on the counter, within easy reach, keep a big container filled with all the utensils you use every day. Organize your cupboards so that glasses, mugs, cutlery and tableware are stored apart from your main work area and the sink, in order to minimize traffic jams when another family member just has to reach for something while you're in the middle of cracking eggs.

WE'RE HERE TO HELP YOU

IN CANADA
HELP LINE
1-800-567-KRAFT
(9 a.m. to 9 p.m. EST,
Monday to Friday)
E-MAIL
kraftkitchens@kraft.com
WEBSITE

kraftcanada.com

IN THE UNITED STATES
HELP LINE
1-877-572-3843 (toll-free)
(9 a.m. to 9 p.m. EST,
Monday to Friday)
E-MAIL
dinner@kraftfoods.com
WEBSITE

kraftfoods.com

If you need help, give us a call.

Not every cookbook comes with a help line, but ours does. Here in the Kraft Kitchens we listen to you and we're here to help with your cooking needs. Monday to Friday, 9 a.m. to 9 p.m. EST, you can call us at the Kraft Kitchens and speak with a food expert on the spot. If you're not sure about a recipe or an ingredient, if you want help with anything in the kitchen, call us and let us give you a hand.

And any time, day or night, you can e-mail us if you prefer – we promise to get back to you promptly during business hours.

Our websites provide all sorts of terrific dinner solutions, tried-and-true recipes, cooking tips and holiday ideas. We also encourage you to join our mailing list and receive recipes by e-mail every week.

Whatever the method, we hope you will be in touch. We'd love to hear from you whenever you have the time.

It's 4 o'clock and someone has just come home feeling hungry. It isn't quite time to start making supper yet. So what can you put on the table that restores energy and fills the gap in a way that satisfies without much time or effort? Here you'll find lots of options, from creamy dips, great nibbling mixes and warm and cheesy tidbits, to frothy, fruity shakes and smoothies. If there are kids in

Snacks & Starters

your kitchen, snack-making can be a lot of fun: Just let them choose from our range of 1-2-3 easy options, then let them do the work of assembling that snack themselves. You'll find you have a few minutes' extra time – to assemble your dinnertime basics or maybe just put your feet up – and it's a great way for kids to gain confidence in the kitchen. It makes them more independent, too, and they're sure to be satisfied with the results if they've done the preparation on their own. To see what the Kraft Kitchens have in mind, turn the page and go.

Munch Mixes   13

Dips and Dippers   14

Cheese and Crackers   21

Shakes and Smoothies   24

Snacktivities for Kids   27

NO-BAKE MUNCH MIX

Just follow our 2 simple steps:
1 MIX together 4 cups unsweetened cereal and a dash of ground cinnamon in a large mixing bowl.
2 ADD 1 cup *each* of chopped mixed dried fruit, toasted almonds and flaked unsweetened coconut; give the mixture a stir. Store in an airtight container.

TEX MIX

Just follow our 3 simple steps:
1 MIX 6 cups unsweetened cereal with 2 cups *each* corn chips and pretzels.
2 TOSS with 1/2 cup melted butter and 1 package (1-1/4 oz) taco seasoning mix; spread on a baking sheet.
3 BAKE at 350°F for 10 minutes, stirring once at the 5-minute mark.

POPCORN CRUNCH

Just follow our 3 simple steps:
1 MIX 6 cups unsweetened cereal with 4 cups popped popcorn.
2 TOSS with 1/2 cup melted butter, 1 tbsp Worcestershire sauce and sprinkle of garlic salt; spread the mixture on a baking sheet.
3 BAKE at 350°F for 10 minutes, giving mixture a stir at the 5-minute mark.

>> **KRAFT KITCHENS TIPS**
Toast your favorite kinds of nuts on a baking sheet in a 300°F oven for 10 to 20 minutes, giving them a stir now and then to keep the toasting even.

Spray your measuring cup lightly with cooking spray before you measure out corn syrup, honey or molasses – you'll find that even the stickiest ingredient slides right out completely.

QUICK VEGETABLE DIPS

CHICKPEA DIP
BLEND 1 can (19 oz) drained chickpeas with 1 or 2 spoonfuls of Italian
or Caesar salad dressing in a blender or food processor.

CUCUMBER DIP
MIX 1 tub (8 oz) Philadelphia Chive & Onion Cream Cheese Spread with
1 cup finely grated cucumber and a pinch of fresh chopped dill.

AVOCADO DIP
MASH 1 ripe avocado and stir in a few spoonfuls of salsa.

SPINACH DIP
Just follow our 2 simple steps:
1 THAW 1 package (10 oz) frozen chopped spinach and squeeze out the
moisture.
2 MIX in 1 cup *each* of Miracle Whip and sour cream.

BROCCOLI DIP
Just follow our 3 simple steps:
1 MICROWAVE 1 package (10 oz) frozen chopped broccoli in a microwavable bowl on HIGH for 3 minutes. Drain.
2 CUBE 1 lb Velveeta and add to broccoli; add a dash of garlic powder
and 1/2 cup sour cream.
3 MICROWAVE on HIGH for 2 to 3 minutes or until Velveeta has
melted. Stir at the halfway mark.

SALSA CHEESE DIP

MIX 2 cups shredded Cheddar cheese with 1/2 cup *each* of sour cream or yogurt and salsa.

COOL DIPS

Just follow our 2 simple steps:

1 COMBINE equal parts Miracle Whip and **cheese** in a bowl.
2 MIX in a handful of **add-ins** and a little **seasoning**.

And use the ingredients you have on hand ...

What **cheese** do you like?	Your favorite **add-ins**	Finish it with **seasoning**
cream cheese spread	canned salmon, drained	1 spoonful of fresh dill
Italian-style shredded cheese	chopped tomato	1 crushed garlic clove
crumbled feta cheese	diced cucumber	1 spoonful of lemon juice
shredded Cheddar cheese	diced tomato	1 or 2 spoonfuls of bacon bits

>> KRAFT KITCHENS TIP
Some vegetables are natural scoops for chunky dips, while other vegetables have lots of nooks and crannies just right for a smoother dip. With thicker dips, we like to serve Belgian endive, celery stalks, chunks of pepper and even carrot coins. With smooth dips, broccoli florets, cauliflower, asparagus and zucchini sticks work well.

Vegetable Partners

>> **KEEP A VARIETY**
of prepared vegetables on
hand to use as an instant
snack while you're preparing
dinner. Set your timer for
30 minutes on a Sunday
afternoon or evening and
you can wash and chop
vegetables to pretty well
see you through the week.

Prepared vegetables in
the fridge also provide
a shortcut when it comes
to making dinner.

Vegetables that taste
better as snacks if they've
been blanched first can
also be prepared ahead
of time in just this way.

BROCCOLI
keeps for 4 days

Blanch pieces in boiling water for 2 minutes, then plunge into cold water to halt cooking. Shake off excess water and refrigerate in a sealed plastic bag.
GOES WITH *Cheez Whiz, tangy tomato-bacon dressing.*

BUTTON MUSHROOMS
keeps for up to 10 days

Refrigerate, unwashed and stored in a paper bag. When you need them, give each a quick rinse and slice off the bottom of the stem end.
GOES WITH *Spinach Dip (page 14), Caesar dressing.*

CARROTS
keeps for 6–7 days

Peel and cut into sticks. Seal in plastic storage container with a little water to keep crisp and refrigerate.
GOES WITH *Broccoli Dip (page 14), ranch dressing.*

CAULIFLOWER
keeps for 4 days

Blanch pieces in boiling water for 4 minutes, then plunge into cold water to halt cooking. Shake off excess water and refrigerate in a sealed plastic bag.
GOES WITH *Cheez Whiz, Caesar dressing.*

CELERY
keeps for 6–7 days

Trim bottoms and tops off celery stalks (reserving trimmings for soup); wash and cut into sticks. Refrigerate in a sealed plastic container with a little water.
GOES WITH *Cheez Whiz, Chickpea Dip (page 14).*

CUCUMBER
keeps for 4–5 days

Wash and slice in half. For field cucumbers, peel and scoop out the seeds. (English ones are fine as is.) Slice into sticks; refrigerate in a sealed plastic bag.
GOES WITH *ranch or cucumber dressing.*

GREEN AND YELLOW BEANS
keeps for 4 days

Blanch in boiling water for 2 minutes, then plunge into cold water to halt cooking. Drain and refrigerate in a sealed plastic bag.
GOES WITH *soy sauce, sour cream.*

PEPPERS
keeps for 4–5 days

Wash whole peppers, then cut off bottom and sides (discarding stem and seeds). Refrigerate in a sealed plastic bag.
GOES WITH *Salsa Cheese Dip (page 17), Caesar dressing, salsa.*

TURNIPS AND RUTABAGAS
keeps for up to 6 days

Trim tops and bottoms, then set on bottom and cut off peel. Cut in half lengthwise, lay on flat side and cut into strips. Refrigerate in a sealed plastic bag.
GOES WITH *applesauce, ranch dressing.*

ZUCCHINI
keeps for 4 days

Wash whole zucchini, trim ends and slice into sticks. Store in refrigerator in a sealed plastic bag.
GOES WITH *creamy Italian dressing.*

MEXICAN PIZZA SNACK

Just follow our 2 simple steps:
1 SPREAD Cheez Whiz on a flour tortilla almost to the edge and add your favorite toppings, such as fresh peppers, jalapeños or leftover chicken, beef or corn.
2 BAKE on a cookie sheet at 400°F for 7 minutes. Cool slightly and cut into wedges.

15-MINUTE NACHOS

Just follow our 2 simple steps:
1 LAYER tortilla chips (or Triscuit crackers, for a change) with 1 chopped tomato, a handful of chopped vegetables and some Kraft Mexican Style Shredded Cheese in a baking dish. (Try any of the following vegetables: olives, jalapeño peppers, zucchini, corn kernels, kidney beans, sweet peppers.)
2 BAKE at 400°F for 8 to 10 minutes.

>> **KRAFT KITCHENS TIP**
Packaged shredded cheese is quick and convenient. If you want to shred your own, make the job easier by first spraying your grater with cooking spray.

QUESADILLAS

Just follow our 3 simple steps:

1 TOP 1 flour tortilla with a handful of shredded **cheese** or with a cheese slice and some sliced **meat**.

2 FOLD tortilla in half; heat 6 minutes over medium heat in a nonstick skillet, turning once at the halfway mark.

3 CUT into 4 pieces and serve with **dipping sauce**.

And use the ingredients you have on hand ...

What **cheese** do you like?	What **meat** is on hand?	A simple **dipping sauce**
Monterey Jack	smoked turkey	1/4 cup sour cream, 1 tsp chili powder, dash of lime juice
process cheese slice	bologna	salsa
Swiss	ham	equal parts mustard and Miracle Whip
Cheddar/mozzarella blend	meatless	applesauce

CHEESE-AND-CRACKER PARTNERS

TRISCUITS
These crackers are the ones to heat. Top with a spoonful of spaghetti sauce and a small piece of mozzarella cheese, or top them with a slice of cheese, a thin slice of apple and a sprinkle of cinnamon sugar instead. Microwave them on HIGH for 8 to 10 seconds – just long enough to melt the cheese on top.

RITZ CRACKERS
Ritz crackers are perfect for spreading. Top with spreadable cream cheese, Cheez Whiz or peanut butter.

WHEAT THINS SNACK CRACKERS
Wheat Thins snack crackers are ideal dipping crackers. Serve them with any of our vegetable-based dips (page 14).

HONEY MAID HONEY GRAHAMS
These crackers are a great partner for all sorts of sliced cheeses. (See the kitchen tip on this page for some of our favorites.)

>> KRAFT KITCHENS TIP
We've found that some of the best cheeses for melting are Havarti, Swiss, Edam, Monterey Jack, Colby and Cheddar, as well as process cheese slices. If you're choosing a cheese to use in a dip, try cream cheese, blue cheese, a cold-pack Cheddar cheese, Velveeta or Cheez Whiz. For slicing, we like to use mild, medium or aged Cheddar, Swiss, brick, Gouda, mozzarella and Monterey Jack.

SHAKES AND SMOOTHIES

>> KRAFT KITCHENS TIP
To clean your blender, make a blender "soap shake." Partly fill your blender jar with hot water and 1 drop of dish detergent. Let the blender run for a couple of minutes, then empty the soapy water, rinse with clean hot water and leave in your drainer to dry.

PEANUT-BUTTER-AND-BANANA SMOOTHIE
BLEND 1 medium-sized banana, 1/2 cup milk and 1 or 2 spoonfuls of peanut butter with 2 ice cubes on HIGH in an electric blender until smooth and frothy.

BERRY CRUSH
BLEND 1 pouch or tub low-calorie lemonade Crystal Light soft drink mix with 3 cups cold skim milk, 1 cup fresh or frozen blueberries and 2 cups ice cubes on HIGH in an electric blender until slushy.

FRUITY SHAKE
BLEND 1/2 tsp unsweetened Kool-Aid drink mix and 2 or 3 spoonfuls of ice cream with 1 cup water on HIGH in an electric blender until smooth.

MELONADE
BLEND equal amounts of cubed cantaloupe and prepared low-calorie tangerine-grapefruit Crystal Light soft drink mix on HIGH in an electric blender until smooth. Serve over ice.

SNACKTIVITIES FOR KIDS

ANTS ON A LOG

CUT celery stalks into 4- to 5-inch pieces, spread inner curve of each piece with Cheez Whiz and top with raisins to make a simple, nutritious treat – with a very funny name.

MEAT-AND-CHEESE DOMINOES

STACK slices of luncheon meat alternately with slices of process cheese, 3 slices high, and cut into small bars the size of dominoes.

PEANUT-BUTTER-AND-BANANA WRAP

SPREAD a flour tortilla on 1 side with peanut butter. Set a peeled banana on top of the peanut butter and roll the tortilla around it.

CHEESE-AND-VEGETABLE KEBABS

ALTERNATE cubes of mozzarella cheese, cherry tomatoes, thick slices of zucchini and chunks of red or green pepper on short wooden skewers.

>> **SHARING OUR EXPERIENCES** Wooden skewers were a huge discovery for me, in terms of feeding my kids. The first time I made Cheese-and-Vegetable Kebabs, my children made it clear they thought I'd made the greatest summer lunch ever. Suddenly, "boring" vegetables were fun to eat. Since then, I've used these skewers with all sorts of ingredients. Even baked chicken fingers are more fun, if you serve them cut into pieces and arranged on skewers just ready to be dunked in barbecue sauce or another dip. —Susanne, Kraft Kitchens

No matter how busy life is, there must always be a little time left at the end of the day for dinner. The challenge on most weeknights, though, is to come up with a variety of great-tasting dishes that are quick and easy to prepare. Here's the time when the family cook wants to make the most of that mental cookbook, relying on winning combinations of everyday ingredients and familiar no-fail

Main Dishes

methods to make evening meals that keep everyone happy. Even the cook. And this is where we really can help you – all you have to do is reach into your cupboards for a few familiar ingredients and we'll show you how to make all sorts of family-pleasing dishes. Tonight and every night. Here you'll find terrific meal ideas that pull together simply in a few minutes' time and clean up like a breeze. At the Kraft Kitchens, we're here to help you find that perfect main dish – every night of the week. Turn the page to see all the great things you can do!

9 x 13s: The Best Baked Casseroles   31

One-Skillet Stovetop Solutions   44

Meat – and Fish – Mainly   58

Everyday Favorites from around the World   75

Sandwiches and Burgers   95

Dinnertime Options with a Personal Touch   111

Main-Dish Vegetables and Greens   120

CHILI BAKE

Just follow our 3 simple steps:

1 MIX together 1/2 cup barbecue sauce, 1 can (19 oz) drained kidney beans, 1-1/2 cups salsa and a spoonful of chili powder.

2 ADD a couple handfuls of frozen mixed vegetables and stir to coat with other ingredients.

3 POUR the mixture over boneless chicken pieces or boneless pork chops (enough for 4) in a baking dish and bake at 375°F for 40 minutes.

>> **KRAFT KITCHENS TIP**

If you're entertaining, dress up this Chili Bake with fresh chopped herbs — a combination of parsley and cilantro is great. Cilantro, also known as coriander or Chinese parsley, is often sold with its roots still attached. If you have the chance, buy cilantro in this form. The roots, finely chopped, add authentic Asian flavor to stir-fries.

OVEN-TENDER BARBECUE BAKES

Just follow our 3 simple steps:

1 PLACE **meat** (1 piece per person should do it) and chopped **veggies** (a handful per person) in a baking dish.

2 ADD 2 cups Kraft Barbecue Sauce and 1 cup of **juice** and toss to coat meat and veggies evenly.

3 BAKE at 400°F for 40 minutes or until meat is completely cooked.

And use the ingredients you have on hand ...

>> TRY THIS, TOO
Serve Oven-Tender Barbecue Bakes with noodles or a rice side dish (see page 152).

Pork Chop Barbecue Bake

What **meat** do you like?	What **veggies** are on hand?	Add this **juice**
chicken pieces	onions, carrots	apple
pork chops	onions, apples	orange
boneless chicken breast	potatoes, onions	pineapple
Italian sausage	onions, peppers	tomato

EVERYDAY EASY RICE DINNERS

Just follow our 3 simple steps:

1 MIX **sauce** and **seasoning** in a 9- x 13-inch baking dish. Add 2 cups Minute White Rice and a couple handfuls of **veggies**.

2 COAT **meat** (1 piece per person should do it) with your favorite variety of Shake'N Bake and place on top of rice.

3 BAKE at 375°F for 35 minutes or until meat is completely cooked.

And use the ingredients you have on hand ...

Chicken Breasts and Broccoli

Pork Chops and Peas

Veal Chops and Mixed Vegetables

What **meat** do you feel like?	Now for the **sauce** and **seasoning**	What **veggies** are on hand?
boneless chicken breasts	1 can (10-3/4 oz) cream of mushroom soup and 2 equal cans of milk; dash of thyme	frozen broccoli
turkey cutlets	1 can (19 oz) stewed tomatoes and equal amount of water	spinach and mushrooms
boneless pork chops	1 can (14 oz) pineapple tidbits and 2 equal cans of water; dash of ground ginger	frozen peas
boneless veal chops	1 can (10-3/4 oz) tomato soup and 2 equal cans of water; dash of mixed herbs	frozen mixed veggies

Turkey Cutlets with Spinach and Mushrooms

PASTA BAKES

Just follow our 3 simple steps:

1 MIX 1 lb cooked **meat** with 3 cups bite-sized uncooked pasta, 2 cups chopped **veggies**, 1 jar (28 oz) spaghetti sauce, a couple handfuls of shredded mozzarella cheese and 1 cup water in a 9- x 13-inch baking dish.

2 SPRINKLE top with more cheese and some dried basil or oregano for extra flavor and cover with foil.

3 BAKE at 400°F for 40 minutes.

And use the ingredients you have on hand …

>> **KRAFT KITCHENS TIP**
The pasta absorbs the water as it bakes. There's no need to precook it.

What **meat** do you feel like?	Add the **veggies**
chicken strips	zucchini
ground beef	peppers
Italian sausage	mushrooms
meatless	mushrooms, peppers, onions

MIX-AND-MATCH POTATO DINNERS

>> **KRAFT KITCHENS TIPS**
If you're starting out with
uncooked meat, microwave
it until done while you
chop the vegetables.

If you have unused
shredded cheese left over,
simply freeze it. Just
add a handful of frozen
cheese to unbaked dishes
and continue with your
preparations.

Just follow our 3 simple steps:

1 MIX 2 cups frozen hash browns and a handful of shredded Cheddar cheese in a 9- x 13-inch baking dish.

2 LAYER with 1 cup *each* of cooked **meat**, your favorite sliced **veggies** and **sauce**. Sprinkle with more cheese.

3 BAKE at 400°F for 30 minutes.

And use the ingredients you have on hand …

What **meat** do you feel like?	What **veggies** are on hand?	Add a **sauce**
boneless, skinless chicken breast	onions, peppers	barbecue sauce
ground beef	corn, green onions	salsa
pepperoni	mushrooms, onions	pizza sauce
meatless	broccoli, zucchini, peppers	canned tomatoes

Ground Beef with Corn and Green Onions

CHEESE STRATA

Just follow our 3 simple steps:

1 PLACE slices of bread in a single layer in a greased 9- x 13-inch baking dish and scatter a handful of chopped vegetables over top. (Frozen vegetables work well in this dish.)

2 BEAT together 6 eggs and 1 cup milk and pour over bread and vegetables so that every slice of bread is completely coated with liquid. Top with a couple handfuls of shredded Cheddar cheese.

3 BAKE at 400°F for 40 minutes or until casserole is cooked through.

>> **TRY THIS, TOO** Cheese Strata works well as a breakfast or brunch casserole. Prepare this dish the night before, cover and refrigerate. Pop in the oven in the morning, 45-50 minutes before it's mealtime, and you're all set.

>> **KRAFT KITCHENS TIP**
If you're unsure about the age of eggs in your fridge, place them in a bowl of cold water. If they sink, they're still fresh; if they float, they're old and should be discarded.

Connecting at Dinnertime

Each day around the same time, families come together for the evening meal. Whether they eat at the kitchen table, in the family room or in a formal dining room, they all share the opportunity to connect with each other over dinner.

At the Kraft Kitchens we've given a lot of thought to what brings people together over food. Some of our ideas are described in the following section. Have a look and see which of these might work around your own dinner table.

PLANNING & PREPARATION

Encourage everyone to help with dinner. Let different family members set the table, wash vegetables or help out with the actual cooking, depending on their skill levels and inclinations.

Sit down as a group to plan a week's worth of meals. You may find that those who've taken part in the menu planning are a lot more likely to enjoy what turns up at mealtime.

Take your kids grocery shopping on a regular basis and involve them in making decisions related to food choices. Help them learn how to look for quality and value.

Make one night a week an international night or a theme dinner and give each family member a turn to pick the weekly theme.

DINNER AS AN EVENT

A few easy house rules turn the dinner hour into a family hour and provide everyone with the opportunity to recharge and reconnect:

Declare the TV set off-limits. Banish newspapers, books and magazines at the dinner table, too.

Use the evening meal to share the events of the day.

Every now and then add flowers or candles to the table, just to make the point that a family is always worth a celebration.

Why not have background music? Let each person in the family take a turn selecting his favorite music. Just make sure that the music doesn't replace family conversation.

As a special perk, provide young table mates with plain paper as place mats and a box of crayons to keep them happy at the table.

Serve breakfast for dinner, as a change. It's a simple twist that appeals to just about everyone.

CLEANUP TIME

Empty the dishwasher before you start to prepare dinner, so that dirty dishes can be loaded immediately after the meal.

Once the food is gone, family members tend to disappear. So why not save dessert until after the dinner table and dishes have been cleaned up?

Rotate cleaning activities for every family member weekly.

ONE-POT RICE DINNERS

Just follow our 3 simple steps:

1 COOK **meat** in a little oil in a large covered nonstick skillet for about 10 minutes – longer for chicken and less time for ham.

2 ADD the **liquid** and 2 cups Minute White Rice (this should be enough for 4). Bring to a boil.

3 STIR in **add-ins**, cover and let stand for 5 minutes.

And use the ingredients you have on hand ...

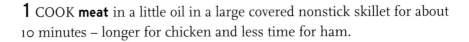

Tuna and Peas

Diced Ham, Pineapple and Pepper

Chicken and Broccoli

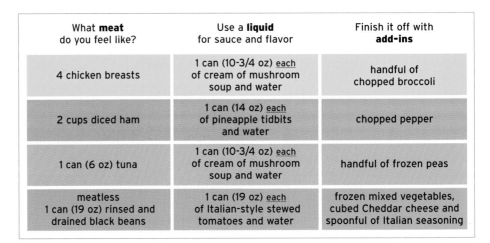

What **meat** do you feel like?	Use a **liquid** for sauce and flavor	Finish it off with **add-ins**
4 chicken breasts	1 can (10-3/4 oz) <u>each</u> of cream of mushroom soup and water	handful of chopped broccoli
2 cups diced ham	1 can (14 oz) <u>each</u> of pineapple tidbits and water	chopped pepper
1 can (6 oz) tuna	1 can (10-3/4 oz) <u>each</u> of cream of mushroom soup and water	handful of frozen peas
meatless 1 can (19 oz) rinsed and drained black beans	1 can (19 oz) <u>each</u> of Italian-style stewed tomatoes and water	frozen mixed vegetables, cubed Cheddar cheese and spoonful of Italian seasoning

Black Beans and Mixed Vegetables with Cheese

THE SIMPLE STIR-FRY

Just follow our 3 simple steps:

1 STIR-FRY sliced **meat** (1 lb should do it for 4) with a bit of Kraft **dressing** for 10 minutes.

2 ADD sliced **veggies** (a handful per person) and cook 10 minutes more.

3 STIR in an additional 1/2 cup dressing to make a sauce. Serve over prepared rice.

And use the ingredients you have on hand ...

>> KRAFT KITCHENS TIP
When buying broccoli, choose a bright green bunch without any yellow discoloration. Fresh broccoli will last 3–4 days in the refrigerator.

What **meat** do you feel like?	What **veggies** are on hand?	Add a **dressing**
chicken breast	cauliflower, peppers, broccoli	sun-dried tomato
beef sirloin	celery, carrots	Italian
pork loin	red cabbage, apples, onions	Catalina
meatless	carrots, broccoli, onions, cauliflower	Italian

Chicken with Cauliflower, Peppers and Broccoli

ZESTY POTATO SOUP

>> **KRAFT KITCHENS TIPS**
Potato varieties differ
in terms of moisture and
starch content. Baking
potatoes are higher
in starch, while boiling
potatoes are higher in
moisture. Standard baking
potatoes work well in
this recipe.

Cutting the Velveeta into
cubes speeds the melting
process.

4 stalks celery
2 <u>each</u> carrots and potatoes
1 <u>each</u> onion and red pepper
5 cups chicken broth
black pepper
1/2 cup <u>each</u> milk and cream
1 lb Velveeta, cut into cubes

1 PEEL and chop vegetables and combine with chicken broth and a dash of pepper in a large saucepan; bring liquid to a boil. Reduce heat and simmer for 15 minutes or until vegetables are tender. Stir occasionally.

2 WHISK in the milk and cream gradually.

3 REDUCE heat to low and add cubed Velveeta. Simmer, stirring, for 5 minutes more or until Velveeta melts and soup is creamy. *Serves 6.*

CHEESY BROCCOLI SOUP

>> **KRAFT KITCHENS TIP**
To save on dishwashing,
use a handheld blender
to purée your soup in the
saucepan. It is a good
idea to let hot items cool
a little before you begin
to blend them.

Just follow our 3 simple steps:

1 COOK 1 large bunch chopped broccoli and 2 chopped carrots with 1 can (10-3/4 oz) *each* chicken broth and water, until vegetables are tender. Let cool 10 minutes.

2 POUR into blender. Process until smooth and return to saucepan.

3 WHISK in 1/2 cup milk and 1 cup Cheez Whiz. Warm over low heat to melt cheese; do not allow the soup to boil.

>> **TRY THIS, TOO** For a more complete meal, add leftover cooked chicken or turkey to this recipe after blending the soup.

CHEESY MINESTRONE SOUP

Just follow our 3 simple steps:
1 PREPARE 1 can (10-3/4 oz) condensed tomato soup according to directions. Bring to boil and add 1/2 cup Minute White Rice; let stand 5 minutes.
2 ADD 1 can (19 oz) drained kidney beans and 1 tsp Italian seasoning.
3 STIR in 2 cups Italian-style shredded cheese. Serve immediately.

HEARTY ONION SOUP

Just follow our 3 simple steps:
1 PREPARE 1 can (10-3/4 oz) condensed onion soup according to directions; add 1 can (28 oz) whole tomatoes with liquid.
2 STIR in 3/4 cup *each* of shredded Swiss and mozzarella cheese.
3 POUR into bowls and top each with 1 slice toasted French bread. Sprinkle with grated Parmesan cheese and additional Swiss and mozzarella cheese.

TEX-MEX CORN CHOWDER

Just follow our 3 simple steps:
1 PREPARE 1 can (10-3/4 oz) condensed cream of mushroom soup; add 4 cut-up wieners, 1 can (12 oz) kernel corn and 1 tsp chili powder.
2 STIR in 2 cups Kraft Mexican Style Shredded Cheese.
3 SERVE with tortilla chips.

>> **KRAFT KITCHENS TIP**
Be sure to give your can opener a cleaning every time you use it, to avoid cross contamination. To clean an electric can opener, brush the cutting mechanism with an old toothbrush dipped in detergent, rinse it off with hot water and then wipe thoroughly with a paper towel.

ONE-POT SAUCY PASTAS

Just follow our 3 simple steps:

1 BROWN **meat** (1 lb should do it for 4) in a large skillet.

2 ADD equal parts pasta sauce, water and uncooked bite-sized pasta (1 cup of *each* per person should do it). Cover, bring to a boil, then reduce heat and simmer for 20 minutes. Add sliced **veggies** (a handful per person), cover and cook 5 minutes more.

3 STIR in a couple handfuls of Italian-style shredded cheese.

And use the ingredients you have on hand …

What **meat** do you feel like?	What **veggies** are on hand?
chicken strips and a few bacon bits	mushrooms
ground beef	mushrooms, onions
diced ham	frozen peas
meatless	mushrooms, onions, broccoli, peppers

>> **KRAFT KITCHENS TIPS**
Your favorite frozen mixed vegetables would be great in any of these variations. For fun, try different shapes of pasta.

A spoonful of pesto or spicy salsa will liven the taste, and you can also add dried or fresh herbs as you like.

One-Pot Saucy Pasta makes great leftovers and it can also be frozen for later use.

Ground Beef with Mushrooms and Onions

LAST-MINUTE PASTAS

>> **KRAFT KITCHENS TIP**
In this recipe, don't worry
about the raw egg. The heat
of the pasta is sufficient to
cook the egg completely.

Just follow our 3 simple steps:

1 BOIL bite-sized pasta (1 cup per person should do it), adding sliced **veggies** (a handful per person) during the last 5 minutes of cooking.

2 DRAIN and return to pot along with a spoonful of **seasoning**.

3 TOSS in the pot over low heat, with 1 beaten egg per person and a handful of shredded mozzarella cheese per person.

And use the ingredients you have on hand …

Broccoli, Carrots and Peppers

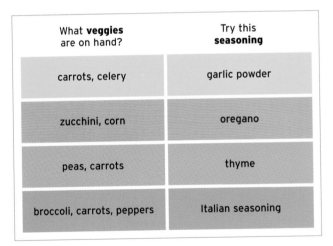

What **veggies** are on hand?	Try this **seasoning**
carrots, celery	garlic powder
zucchini, corn	oregano
peas, carrots	thyme
broccoli, carrots, peppers	Italian seasoning

Carrots and Celery with Bow-Tie Pasta

EVERYDAY EASY MACARONI DINNERS

Just follow our 3 simple steps:

1 COOK **meat** in a nonstick skillet. Add 2 cups *each* of water and macaroni, with 1 cup of milk and a spoonful of butter. Cook over medium heat until macaroni is soft, stirring frequently to prevent scorching.

2 ADD 2 cups **Kraft Shredded Cheese** and a few spoonfuls of grated Parmesan cheese. Stir until melted.

3 STIR in **add-ins** and top with more cheese.

And use the ingredients you have on hand …

What **meat** do you feel like?	Try this **Kraft Shredded Cheese**	And now for the **add-ins**
1 lb chopped boneless, skinless chicken	Italian Style	small can (19 oz) drained stewed tomatoes, dash of thyme
1 lb ground beef	Mexican Style	few spoonfuls of salsa, dash of chili powder
1 can (6 oz) tuna	Cheddar	sliced celery, dash of Italian seasoning
meatless	mozzarella/Cheddar	chopped green onions, few spoonfuls of salsa

>> **SHARING OUR EXPERIENCES**
This dish is a classic example of "un-doing" a time-consuming traditional recipe. By cooking everything in one pot and thickening the sauce with flavorful cheese rather than the usual white sauce (which takes time to prepare), we've taken a weekend favorite and made it perfect for any night of the week.
—Michele, Kraft Kitchens

MASTER MEATBALLS MIXTURE

>> **KRAFT KITCHENS TIP**
Bake a batch of these meatballs in advance and store
them in your freezer.
Our Saucy Meatball Supper
also can be made ahead
of time and stored in a
freezer bag until needed.

Just follow our 3 simple steps:
1 COMBINE 1 lb extra-lean ground beef with 1/2 cup *each* of bread crumbs and barbecue sauce, 1 egg and a few spoonfuls of grated Parmesan cheese.
2 ROLL into even-sized balls and place on baking sheet.
3 BAKE at 400°F for 20 minutes, until meatballs are cooked through.

Master Meatballs are terrific in the following ways:

LAST-MINUTE MONSTER MEATBALL SANDWICH
1 COOK your favorite vegetables (try onions, peppers and mushrooms) in a skillet with a bit of oil. Add cooked meatballs, as many as you like, and barbecue sauce – enough to coat all the ingredients. Cook until meatballs are warmed through.
2 PLACE meatballs and vegetables in an open Italian-style bun; sprinkle with shredded Cheddar cheese. Place under broiler just until cheese melts.

SAUCY MEATBALL SUPPER
1 MIX 1 cup *each* of spicy barbecue sauce and your favorite frozen juice concentrate (thawed). Add 1 tbsp soy sauce and a pinch of ground ginger.
2 POUR over cooked meatballs – about 4 or 5 per person – and heat through in a skillet over medium-high heat. Serve over rice.

Saucy Meatball Supper

ORANGE PORK BAKE

Just follow our 3 simple steps:

1 ARRANGE 6 boneless pork chops in a casserole dish. Sprinkle 1 envelope dry onion soup mix over top.

2 MIX 1/2 cup *each* of French dressing and orange juice and pour over the chops. Top with 3 peeled and sliced oranges.

3 BAKE at 400°F for 40 minutes.

>> **KRAFT KITCHENS TIPS**
Dress up your Orange Pork Bake with a splash of wine in the pan or use navel or blood oranges for more intense color, and you'll have a dish that's perfect for entertaining.

Try this dish with rice pilaf, a bowl of Minute White Rice made with orange juice instead of water and topped with toasted almonds, or one of our other tried-and-true rice ideas (page 152).

ONE-PAN DINNER BAKES

Just follow our 3 simple steps:

1 COAT **meat** or eggplant (1 piece per person should do it) with your favorite variety of Shake'N Bake. Place in a 9- x 13-inch baking dish.

2 ADD sliced **veggies** (a handful per person) and sprinkle with Italian dressing.

3 BAKE at 400°F for 30 minutes, then top each piece of meat or eggplant with a spoonful of **sauce** and some shredded mozzarella cheese. Bake for 5 minutes more to melt the cheese.

And use the ingredients you have on hand …

Chicken with Carrots and Celery

Eggplant with Zucchini

Pork Chops with Potato Wedges

What **meat** do you feel like?	What **veggies** are on hand?	Top with **sauce**
boneless chicken breast	carrots, celery	pizza sauce
turkey breast	peppers	salsa
boneless pork chops	potato and sweet potato wedges	barbecue sauce
meatless (try slices of eggplant)	zucchini, onions	pasta sauce

Turkey Breast with Peppers and Salsa

Chicken Know-How

>> **KRAFT KITCHENS TIP**
Cook chicken until it is well done: It should not be eaten "rare" or "medium." When completely cooked chicken is pierced with a fork, the juices run clear and you won't see any tinge of pink. The internal temperature of cooked chicken pieces should read 170°F on your meat thermometer; a whole roast chicken should reach 180°F and cooked ground chicken should read 175°F when fully cooked.

CHICKEN CUTS

Boneless, skinless breasts are excellent for quick-cooking food ideas such as grilled chicken sandwiches, kebabs and grilled salads.

Bone-in pieces such as quarter chicken legs take longer to cook than boneless pieces.

Tender, flavorful dark meat – from the legs and thighs – is offered at a more economical price because there is a greater demand for white meat. Dark meat is very moist and contains more fat than white meat, which means that it is better able to withstand the intense heat of a grill.

Strips of dark meat are especially good for fajitas and stir-fries.

Leftover cooked dark meat is excellent in soups and stews.

HANDLING CHICKEN

First and foremost, never buy chicken without checking the sell-by date on the package to be certain the chicken is fresh.

Always refrigerate raw chicken on the bottom shelf of the refrigerator to ensure that it doesn't drip on any other food.

After handling raw chicken, wash your hands thoroughly in hot, soapy water. Do the same with any utensils or containers that have come into contact with the raw chicken.

Defrost frozen chicken in the refrigerator, rather than allowing it to defrost at room temperature.

FREEZING CHICKEN

You can safely freeze whole chickens for up to 1 year, raw chicken parts for up to 9 months, cooked chicken parts for up to 4 months and ground chicken for no more than 3 months.

If you freeze chicken pieces with Italian salad dressing in sealable plastic bags, the chicken will marinate as it thaws.

If you are planning to prepare a recipe that calls for sliced chicken, you'll find the chicken slices more easily before it is thawed completely.

COOKING METHODS

Brown chicken over medium heat in a skillet. (High heat can turn the outer edge of the meat stringy.)

To ensure a crisp, deep golden brown skin on your roast chicken, rub the surface with regular – not light – mayonnaise before the bird goes in the oven.

>> KRAFT KITCHENS TIP

Never cover chicken with plastic wrap for cooking in the microwave. The plastic wrap holds in too much moisture, stewing meat and turning it stringy. Instead, loosely cover chicken with waxed paper to prevent spatters and maintain even heat.

MIX-AND-MATCH CHICKEN BAKES

>> **KRAFT KITCHENS TIPS**
You can also use boneless, skinless chicken breasts in this dish. Just reduce the baking time to 30 minutes.

Add other quick-cooking vegetables, including left-over potatoes, frozen mixed vegetables and zucchini, if you like.

Just follow our 3 simple steps:

1 PLACE **meat** (1 piece per person should do it), thinly sliced potatoes and onions with sliced **fruit/veggies** (a couple handfuls of each) in a baking dish.

2 COMBINE **sauce** ingredients (1/2 cup of *each* should do it) and pour the mixture over chicken.

3 BAKE, uncovered, at 400°F for 45 minutes or until chicken and vegetables are completely cooked.

And use the ingredients you have on hand …

What **meat** do you feel like?	What **fruit/veggies** are on hand?	Add a **sauce**
bone-in chicken breast halves	apples	barbecue sauce, apple juice
chicken thighs	peppers	Miracle Whip, spaghetti sauce
bone-in chicken breast halves	green beans	Kraft Catalina Dressing, marmalade
quarter chicken legs	carrots	Miracle Whip, frozen orange juice concentrate

Chicken Thighs with Peppers

MASTER CRISPY CHICKEN COATING

>> TRY THIS, TOO
Simple side dishes such as Philly Mashed Potatoes (page 144), stuffing with add-ins (page 153) or a steamed vegetable with Cheez Whiz topping (page 139) all go well with Crispy Chicken.

Just follow our 3 simple steps:

1 MOISTEN 6 to 8 pieces of boneless chicken with water. Shake off excess.

2 SHAKE 1 or 2 pieces at a time with 1 packet Shake'N Bake. Place coated chicken pieces in a baking dish lined with foil, discarding any unused coating mix.

3 BAKE at 400°F for 20 minutes or until chicken pieces are completely cooked.

>> SHARING OUR EXPERIENCES Crispy Coconut Curry Chicken is a favorite of mine. Originally, I used this method on shrimp, and then I thought why not try it with chicken fingers? The combination of crumbs, coconut and curry not only provides that crispness but it also holds in all the juices of the chicken.
—Maxine, Kraft Kitchens

Coated Crispy Chicken is terrific in the following ways:

>> **KRAFT KITCHENS TIP**
Freeze pieces of chicken, steak and pork in individual plastic bags. They'll thaw more quickly and it's easier to pull out one or several from the freezer, depending on what you require.

HOT-AND-SPICY CRISPY CHICKEN

Follow basic recipe, adding 1/2 to 1 tsp crushed red pepper flakes to the coating mix. (If you like your chicken really hot, add a little more.)

CHEESY CRISPY CHICKEN

Follow basic recipe. After baking, top each chicken piece with a slice of process cheese and return to oven for an additional 3 minutes or until cheese has melted.

EXTRA-CRISPY PARMESAN CHICKEN

Follow basic recipe, adding 1/2 cup grated Parmesan cheese to the coating mix.

ALMOND CHICKEN

Follow basic recipe, adding 1/4 cup ground almonds and a spoonful of ground ginger to the coating mix.

CRISPY COCONUT-CURRY CHICKEN

Follow basic recipe, adding 1/4 cup shredded coconut and 1 or 2 tsp curry powder to the coating mixture before you shake the chicken. You can also use a few drops of hot sauce to moisten chicken before coating it.

HOMEMADE CHICKEN FINGERS

Just follow our 3 simple steps:
1 CUT 5 to 6 boneless, skinless chicken breasts into strips or cubes.
2 EMPTY 1 packet Shake'N Bake into shaker bag. Moisten chicken with water and shake off excess. Shake chicken in coating mix, to coat evenly.
3 PLACE chicken pieces on foil-lined 9- x 13-inch baking dish and bake at 400°F for 10–15 minutes.

SHAKE'N BAKE SPICY BARBECUE WINGS

Just follow our 3 simple steps:
1 CUT 2 lb fresh or thawed chicken wings at joints and discard tips.
2 EMPTY 1 packet of spicy-wing Shake'N Bake into the shaker bag. Moisten wings with water, shaking off excess, and shake 3 or 4 pieces at a time.
3 PLACE on a foil-lined baking sheet. Sprinkle remaining coating mix evenly over wings and bake at 350°F for 40 to 45 minutes.

>> TRY THIS, TOO
Eat-with-your-fingers nights can be a lot of fun for everyone. Along with these Homemade Chicken Fingers or Spicy Barbecue Wings, why not serve raw vegetables and a creamy vegetable dip (page 14)?

To complete the theme, our Peanut-Butter Fruit Dip (page 178) served with fresh fruit would make a great end to the meal.

OVEN-BAKED FISH AND CHIPS

>> **KRAFT KITCHENS TIP**
Frozen fish should be solid,
free of ice crystals and
show no white spots (an
indication of freezer burn).
Packages should be clean
and tightly sealed.

Just follow our 3 simple steps:
1 SHAKE 1 block frozen fish in Shake'N Bake.
2 PLACE on a foil-lined baking sheet along with a package of frozen potato wedges or fries.
3 BAKE at 450°F for 20 minutes or until fish flakes easily with a fork.

SAUCY MICROWAVE FISH SUPPER

Just follow our 3 simple steps:
1 MIX 1 can (10-3/4 oz) *each* of condensed cream of mushroom soup and water with 1-1/2 cups Minute White Rice. Top with individual frozen fish fillets (1 per person should do it) and cover.
2 MICROWAVE on HIGH for 15 minutes or until fish flakes easily with a fork.
3 TOP with shredded Cheddar cheese and let stand for 5 minutes.

Saucy Microwave Fish Supper

QUICK JAMBALAYA

Just follow our 3 simple steps:

1 HEAT a spoonful of oil in a large skillet and sauté 1 *each* chopped onion, pepper and garlic clove until tender-crisp.

2 ADD 1 can (19 oz) chili-style stewed tomatoes, 1 can (10-3/4 oz) chicken broth and a handful of chopped cooked ham. Bring to a boil.

3 STIR in 1-1/2 cups Minute White Rice, 1/4 cup barbecue sauce and a few handfuls of thawed precooked frozen shrimp. Bring to a boil, cover pan, remove from heat and let stand for 5 to 10 minutes.

CAJUN DIRTY RICE

Just follow our 3 simple steps:

1 BROWN 1 lb ground beef and 1 chopped onion in a large saucepan.

2 ADD 1 can (10-3/4 oz) chicken broth, 1 *each* chopped pepper and celery stalk, 1 large spoonful of chili powder and 1 small spoonful of ground cumin and dried parsley. Bring the mixture to a boil.

3 ADD 1-1/2 cups Minute White Rice and 2 chopped green onions. Cover and let stand 5 to 10 minutes or until rice is tender.

>> **KRAFT KITCHENS TIP**
What makes Dirty Rice "dirty?" Traditionally, the dish is made with ground turkey, or chicken gizzards and livers, which gives the rice its characteristic dirty appearance.

SEASONED COLLARD GREENS

>> KRAFT KITCHENS TIP
Greens are an essential part of the southern diet in the U.S. Many of us are familiar with spinach, but what about kale, mustard and collard greens? All of these are widely available at grocery stores, and yet they are often overlooked. To prepare, gently cook them with a little butter and some stock or stir-fry them in a small amount of butter until they are wilted and tender or steam them in the microwave.

3 lb fresh collard greens
4 slices bacon
1 medium chopped onion
2 minced garlic cloves
2 cups water
1 tsp sugar
1/2 tsp red pepper flakes
1/4 tsp salt

1 WASH greens, removing all grit. Remove stems. Place greens in small bunches; roll up. Cut crosswise into wide strips.

2 CHOP bacon and cook in a large skillet over medium heat; remove cooked bacon with a slotted spoon. Drain skillet, reserving just 1 tbsp drippings in the bottom. Add onion and garlic to pan and cook over medium heat, stirring frequently, until vegetables are tender.

3 ADD greens, water, sugar, red pepper flakes and salt. Simmer on low heat for 45 minutes to 1 hour or until greens are soft and tender. Stir in reserved bacon and serve. *Serves 4.*

PICKLED BLACK-EYED PEAS

>> **TRY THIS, TOO**
Purchase your favorite
fried chicken to serve
with Seasoned Collard
Greens, Pickled Black-
Eyed Peas, Praline Sweet
Potatoes and/or Southern-
style Cornbread for
a meal.

2 cans (16 oz <u>each</u>) rinsed and drained black-eyed peas
1 small chopped onion
1/4 cup <u>each</u> chopped green and red pepper
1 tbsp minced garlic
1/2 cup zesty Italian dressing
1 head Boston lettuce, separated into 8 leaves

1 TOSS together peas, onions, peppers and garlic in a bowl.

2 ADD dressing and mix together lightly. Cover and refrigerate several hours or overnight, stirring occasionally.

3 ARRANGE lettuce leaves on salad plates and spoon black-eyed peas over top. *Serves 4.*

PRALINE SWEET POTATOES

Just follow our 3 simple steps:

1 BOIL 3 to 4 chopped, peeled sweet potatoes for 15 to 20 minutes or until the potatoes are completely tender; drain.

2 MASH sweet potatoes with 1/2 cup butter, 1 tsp *each* of ground ginger and grated orange peel and 1/2 tsp of ground cinnamon.

3 TRANSFER mashed sweet potatoes to baking dish. Top with pecans and bake at 350°F for 30 minutes.

SOUTHERN-STYLE CORNBREAD

Just follow our 3 simple steps:

1 MIX together 1 cup cornmeal, 1/2 cup flour, 3 tbsp brown sugar, 2 tsp baking powder and a dash of salt in a large bowl.

2 ADD 1 can (8 oz) creamed corn, 1/4 cup vegetable oil, 1 egg, 2 chopped green onions and 1/2 red pepper, chopped, and stir with dry ingredients just until combined.

3 POUR into a greased 8-inch square baking pan. Bake at 400°F for 20 to 25 minutes. Cut into squares and serve warm.

>> KRAFT KITCHENS TIP

Looking for another idea for sweet potatoes? Some particularly good partners include pineapple, oranges, apples and pecans. In the southwestern U.S. and Mexico you may find sweet potatoes perked up with chili peppers, cilantro, scallion, tomato, garlic, lemon and lime, as well.

MUCHOS TACOS MASTER MIXTURE

>> **KRAFT KITCHENS TIP**
To make tortilla cups, invert
four 10-oz custard cups on
a baking pan. Spray outside
of each with nonstick spray.
Place a tortilla over each
cup and bake at 450°F for
5 minutes or until light
brown — so they hold shape
when turned right side up.

Noodle Taco Bowls

Just follow our 2 simple steps:
1 BROWN 1 lb ground beef in a skillet; drain fat, leaving meat in pan.
2 ADD 1 package (1-1/4 oz) taco seasoning mix and 3/4 cup water. Bring mixture to a boil; reduce heat and simmer for 10 minutes, stirring occasionally.

Muchos Tacos Mixture is terrific in the following ways:

NOODLE TACO BOWLS
1 ADD 2-1/2 cups water to master meat mixture. Bring to a boil.
2 MIX in dry macaroni from 1 package (7-1/4 oz) Kraft Macaroni & Cheese Dinner. Reduce heat, cover and simmer for 7 minutes or until macaroni is tender, stirring occasionally. Stir in cheese-sauce mix.
3 STIR in 1 *each* chopped tomato and green onion and a handful of sliced black olives. Serve in tortilla cups (see tip), or use tortilla chips as a base.

DOUBLE-DECKER TACOS
1 WARM small flour tortillas and spread them with a spoonful of hot refried beans. Set 1 crisp taco shell in the center; fold flour tortillas over the shells.
2 FILL taco shells with hot master meat mixture and then top with Kraft Mexican Style Shredded Cheese, sour cream, chopped tomato and lettuce and a spoonful of salsa. Serve immediately.

Double-Decker Tacos

CHEESY BURRITOS

Just follow our 3 simple steps:

1 BROWN 1 lb **meat** and a handful (per person) of **veggies** over medium-high heat. Drain off fat. Stir in 1/2 cup salsa and 1 cup of **Kraft Shredded Cheese**.

2 SPREAD 1 cup salsa in a 9- x 13-inch baking dish. Spoon 1/4 cup meat mixture down center of each of 10 small flour tortillas and roll up. Place each rolled tortilla, seam side down, on top of salsa. Top with more salsa and cheese.

3 BAKE at 350°F for 20 minutes or until the burritos are heated through.

And use the ingredients you have on hand ...

What **meat/veggies** do you feel like?	What **Kraft Shredded Cheese** is on hand?
chicken, cut into strips	Mexican Style
ground beef	Cheddar
meatless (refried beans)	mozzarella/Cheddar
meatless (peppers and onions)	mozzarella

QUICK PAELLA

>> **KRAFT KITCHENS TIP**

In Spain, paella is often cooked outside over an open fire. Traditional paella — cooked in a special low two-handled pan — is flavored with saffron, which gives the rice a beautiful rich color. Turmeric provides the color in our version. You can find many variations of paella, all with different combinations of meats and/or seafood.

1/2 lb hot Italian sausage
1/2 lb boneless, skinless chicken breasts
1 medium chopped onion
2 minced garlic cloves
1 diced green pepper
1 can (19 oz) diced tomatoes
1 can (10-3/4 oz) chicken broth
1 cup frozen peas
1 tsp <u>each</u> red chili pepper flakes and turmeric
2-1/2 cups Minute White Rice
1 package frozen precooked shrimp, thawed
Juice of 1 lemon

1 CUT sausage and chicken into chunks. Sauté in a large skillet, with onion, garlic and pepper until just cooked.

2 ADD remaining ingredients except rice, shrimp and lemon juice. Bring to a boil.

3 STIR in rice and shrimp; return to a boil. Cover, remove from heat and let stand 5 to 10 minutes. Top with fresh lemon juice just before serving. *Serves 4.*

Asian Know-How

Noodles have long been a staple throughout the Far East and Southeast Asia. They can be made from wheat, rice, beans, tapioca, soybeans and even seaweed.

In the Chinese culture, noodles symbolize longevity – it's their length that's symbolic – and they are always served at birthdays to represent the wish for a long life.

A wok is the main cooking vessel in an Asian kitchen. If you're shopping for a wok, choose one that is at least 12 inches in diameter. If you don't have a wok, a large, deep skillet will work instead: Just remember to keep the food moving in the pan as you stir-fry.

Garlic, ginger and green onions are indispensable ingredients in Asian cooking. Use a lot and use them often.

Shallots, garlic and ginger, bird's eye chili peppers, cilantro and fish sauce are essential ingredients in a traditional Thai pantry.

Bird's eye chili peppers may be small, but they pack a lot of heat. To prevent severe skin irritation, be sure to wear rubber gloves when cutting them and wash your hands thoroughly when you are through.

Sesame oil is made of pressed toasted sesame seeds. It has a delicious aromatic smell and a nutty flavor. Sesame oil isn't used for cooking because it breaks down so easily. Instead of adding it over heat, drizzle sesame oil over your finished dishes just prior to serving. Purchase it in small bottles – it is used sparingly – and store in the refrigerator to keep it tasting fresh.

>> **KRAFT KITCHENS TIP**
Soy sauce is made of fermented soybeans and there are light and dark versions available. Of the two, dark soy sauce is slightly sweeter, but both have a distinctive taste and are quite salty. Store soy sauce in a cool, dark place or in the refrigerator.

EASY ASIAN NOODLE DINNERS

Just follow our 3 simple steps:

1 BROWN sliced **meat** (1 lb should do it for 4) in 2 tbsp Kraft Catalina Dressing. Add sliced **veggies/fruit** (a handful per person) and cook 10 minutes more.

2 ADD another 1/2 cup dressing and **add-ins**.

3 ADD thin noodles – 4 oz for 4 – breaking them in half, if necessary, to fit them in the pan. Cover, bring to a boil; reduce heat and simmer for 10 minutes, stirring frequently.

And use the ingredients you have on hand ...

Sirloin with Carrots and Celery

Chicken with Stir-Fry Vegetables

Mixed Vegetable

What **meat** do you feel like?	What **veggies/fruit** are on hand?	Now for the **add-ins**
chicken	frozen stir-fry veggies	1 cup chicken broth, spoonful of curry powder
sirloin steak	carrots, celery	1 cup beef broth, 2 tbsp teriyaki sauce
ham	1 can (14 oz) pineapple tidbits (juice reserved), peppers	reserved pineapple juice, a few dashes of ground ginger
meatless	frozen mixed veggies	1 cup water, 1/4 cup vinegar and a few drops of hot sauce

Ham with Pineapple and Peppers

PEANUT-SESAME STIR-FRY

1 cup Kraft Catalina Dressing
1/4 cup peanut butter
3 tbsp <u>each</u> soy sauce and lemon juice
2 tbsp sesame seeds
1 lb peeled shrimp
1 can (10 oz) drained, sliced water chestnuts
3 sliced green onions
1 cubed zucchini
1 <u>each</u> cubed green and red pepper
1 can (10 oz) drained mandarin orange segments
Cooked noodles

1 MIX together dressing, peanut butter, soy sauce and lemon juice.

2 STIR-FRY sesame seeds and shrimp in one-third of the prepared sauce in a wok or a heavy skillet.

3 ADD remaining ingredients except for mandarin orange segments and noodles; cook until vegetables are tender. Add mandarin orange segments and the remaining sauce. Serve over noodles. *Serves 4.*

>> **KRAFT KITCHENS TIPS**
Shrimp take only a few minutes to cook and they're done as soon as they turn pink. If you overcook them, they will become rubbery.

If you are using frozen precooked shrimp, thaw them first. The best way to do this is to place them in a colander and run cold water over them for a few minutes.

ONE-POT CURRY-AND-RICE DINNERS

>> **KRAFT KITCHENS TIPS**

An authentic curry may
contain as many as
20 spices that have been
ground together in a
precise combination. (In
our One-Pot Curries, we
streamline the process
by using only pre-blended
curry powder, plus one
other common household
spice per variation.)

Spicier dishes generally
are served with a yogurt-
based sauce to cool the
mouth. In this recipe,
a creamy dressing serves
the same purpose.

Just follow our 3 simple steps:

1 MIX 1/2 cup creamy cucumber or ranch dressing with 1 to 2 tbsp curry powder, pour over sliced **meat** (1 lb for 4) and marinate for 10 minutes.
2 COOK marinated meat, a handful *each* of chopped celery, green onion and carrots until they brown. Pour in 1 can (10-3/4 oz) broth and an equal amount of Minute White Rice; bring to a boil.
3 REMOVE from heat, stir in a handful *each* of your chosen **add-in** and nuts such as peanuts, cashews, toasted almonds or sunflower seeds. Add your **seasoning**. Cover and let stand for 10 minutes.

And use the ingredients you have on hand . . .

What **meat** do you feel like?	What **add-ins** are on hand?	Now for the **seasoning**
chicken	dried diced apricots	2 tsp ground ginger
beef	diced apples	1 tsp chili powder
pork	shredded coconut	1 tsp ground cloves
meatless	raisins	1 tsp hot pepper sauce

Chicken with Apricots

WARM HANDHELD SANDWICHES

Just follow our 3 simple steps:

1 SLICE 2 buns in half, lengthwise. Hollow out the interiors by hand.

2 MIX 1/2 cup Kraft Mayo with a handful of shredded cheese and a couple spoonfuls of **add-ins**. Spread sauce on the hollowed-out insides of the buns.

3 LAYER with thinly sliced deli **meat** and sliced **fillings**, repeating until filled just above the top of the bun. Replace the tops and wrap each sandwich in foil. Bake at 400°F for 15 minutes. Unwrap, slice and serve immediately.

And use the ingredients you have on hand ...

What deli **meat** do you feel like?	What **add-ins** are on hand?	Now for the **fillings**
chicken	chili powder	green onions, chunky salsa
roast beef	barbecue sauce	black olives, roasted peppers
ham	teriyaki sauce	green peppers, drained pineapple tidbits
salami	Cheez Whiz	mushrooms, dill pickles

>> **KRAFT KITCHENS TIP**
Keep some of the following in your pantry and you'll always have variety for those last-minute sandwiches: bottled roasted peppers, dill pickles, black olives, salsa, pineapple tidbits and barbecue sauce.

Ham, Pineapple and Peppers

Chicken with Salsa and Green Onions

MEAL-IN-ONE DINNER SANDWICHES

>> **KRAFT KITCHEN TIPS**
Wrap single-serving left-over sandwich wedges in plastic wrap and freeze or refrigerate.

For thorough cooking, slice vegetables as thinly as possible.

Just follow our 3 simple steps:

1 SLICE a 1/2-inch-thick cap off a round loaf of bread, hollow out the interior by hand and place your chosen **spread** on inside bottom, sides and cap.

2 LAYER deli **meat** (1/4 lb per loaf should do it), **veggies** and shredded mozzarella cheese. Replace the cap and wrap the loaf in aluminum foil.

3 HEAT at 400°F for 30 minutes or until cheese has melted. Let stand 10 minutes before cutting into wedges with a serrated knife. Serve immediately.

And use the ingredients you have on hand . . .

Turkey with Spinach

What deli **meat** do you feel like?	What **spread** is on hand?	Now for the **veggies**
turkey	mayonnaise	spinach, dried cranberries, onions
pepperoni	pizza sauce	mushrooms, onions, peppers
ham	Dijon mustard	tomatoes, onions
meatless	pesto sauce	mushrooms, artichokes, roasted peppers

Mushroom, Artichoke and Roasted Pepper Meal-in-One

10 WAYS WITH GRILLED CHEESE

MASTER SANDWICH RECIPE
SPREAD each side of 2 slices of bread with butter. Place Kraft Singles in between the slices of bread and cook in a nonstick skillet over medium heat until the exterior is golden – about 3 minutes per side.

SALSA-AND-TURKEY GRILLED CHEESE
ADD 2 slices of deli roast turkey and a spoonful of salsa before cooking.

GRILLED CHEESE WITH BACON
ADD 3 slices cooked bacon to your sandwich before cooking.

GRILLED CHEESE WITH ONIONS
ADD Dijon mustard and a little sautéed onion on top, then cover with Kraft Singles; top with second slice of bread and cook.

DOUBLE GRILLED CHEESE
ADD an extra Kraft Swiss or mozzarella Singles slice before cooking.

TOMATO GRILLED CHEESE
USE rye bread and add slices of tomato before cooking.

PICKLED GRILLED CHEESE
ADD sliced bread-and-butter or sandwich-sliced dill pickles before cooking.

GRILLED GRAPE SANDWICH
ADD sliced green or red grapes to your filling before cooking. (*More ...*)

>> **SHARING OUR EXPERIENCES**
It may sound crazy, but the Grilled Grape Sandwich is amazing. My children inspired us all to try it and now it's a Kraft Kitchens favorite, as well.
—Karen, Kraft Kitchens

Add flavor and zip to grilled cheese sandwiches – with only half the calories of butter – by brushing the bread with light mayonnaise instead of butter.

If you want to make grilled cheese sandwiches for a crowd, fill a baking sheet with prepared sandwiches and broil them for 5 minutes per side.

Just wrap leftovers in plastic wrap and refrigerate. They're great cold, too – even for breakfast.

And for the more adventurous …

GRILLED CHEESE-AND-VEGETABLE PITA

1 CUT a round of pita bread into 2 half circles and fill each pocket with slices of tomato and chopped grilled vegetables, such as onion, mushroom and red and green peppers.
2 ADD Kraft Singles to each half.
3 GRILL in a hot skillet over medium heat until pita is golden brown and cheese is melted – about 3 minutes per side.

GRILLED CHEESE-AND-HAM MONTE CRISTO

1 TOP 1 slice rye bread with 1 deli slice cooked ham and 1 Kraft Singles. Cover with second slice of bread.
2 BEAT 1 egg in a shallow dish. Dip sandwich in egg to coat on either side.
3 GRILL in hot skillet that has been greased with nonstick cooking spray, over medium heat, until bread is golden brown and cheese is melted.

CHEESE-AND-APPLE ON RAISIN BREAD

1 SPREAD 2 slices of raisin bread with butter.
2 PLACE Kraft Singles and 4 thin slices of apple in between the 2 pieces of bread.
3 GRILL in hot skillet over medium heat until bread is golden brown and cheese is melted – about 2 minutes per side.

CLUB ON A BUN

Just follow our 2 simple steps:

1 CUT 1 onion or cheese bun into 3 slices horizontally. Toast.

2 SPREAD 1 side of each slice with Kraft Mayo. Place lettuce, sliced tomato, sliced turkey or ham and 2 slices process cheese on bottom slice of bun. Top with middle slice; repeat layers using cooked bacon instead of turkey. Add top section of bun and serve.

>> TRY THIS, TOO
Serve our Club on a Bun sandwich with Potato Wedges and Peppers (page 143). Hot Pizza Bread is terrific with a simple Caesar salad.

HOT PIZZA BREAD

Just follow our 3 simple steps:

1 CUT 1 loaf French bread into 1-inch slices, cutting only three-quarters of the way through the loaf with each slice. Spread a spoonful of pizza or pasta sauce into each cut and tuck a few slices of pepperoni and thin strips of pepper in as well.

2 SPRINKLE loaf with 1/2 cup grated Parmesan cheese and 1 cup shredded mozzarella cheese.

3 WRAP loaf in aluminum foil and bake at 400°F for 15 minutes.

EASY DINNER MELTS

>> **KRAFT KITCHENS TIPS**
With our Easy Dinner Melts, these last-minute toppings are perfect: dill pickles, sliced avocado, lettuce, and tomato.

If you're just making 1 or 2 of these sandwiches, why not use your toaster oven?

Egg and Cheddar

Just follow our 3 simple steps:

1 COMBINE chopped cooked **meat** with a couple spoonfuls of Miracle Whip, a few handfuls of shredded **cheese** and some **add-ins**. Spread on a favorite type of bread, such as a cheese bun, some French bread, a bagel, a pizza shell or a tortilla.

2 BAKE at 400°F for 20 minutes.

3 ADD extra toppings (see our kitchen tip) and serve.

And use the ingredients you have on hand . . .

What **meat** do you feel like tonight?	What **cheese** is on hand?	Now for the **add-ins**
chicken	Mexican-style	sliced green onion and salsa
turkey	mozzarella	chopped green onion
ham	Italian-style	chopped pickle
hard-cooked egg	Cheddar	pinch of dry mustard

Ham-and-Pickle Dinner Melt

HOT-AND-CHEESY PULL-APARTS

Just follow our 3 simple steps:

1 MIX 1/2 cup Kraft Mayo and 1/4 cup Italian dressing.

2 CUT ends off bread to make a 12-inch loaf. Slice bread evenly into 12 slices, taking care not to cut all the way through to the bottom of the loaf so that all the slices remain connected. In every space, spread a bit of the mayonnaise/dressing mixture and then fit in **sliced cooked meat**, **veggies** and sliced **cheese**.

3 BAKE at 350°F for 15 to 20 minutes or until cheese melts and loaf is hot.

And use the ingredients you have on hand …

>> KRAFT KITCHENS TIP
Foil-wrapped (unheated) pull-apart loaves transport well. If you're including tomato slices, add these when you reach your destination, just before heating the loaf. Seed your tomatoes, to prevent sogginess.

What **sliced cooked meat** do you feel like?	What **veggies** are on hand?	Now for the **cheese**
turkey	mushrooms	Havarti
roast beef	onions	Swiss
ham	tomatoes	process cheese slices
meatless	peppers, tomatoes, onions	Cheddar

MASTER BURGER MIXTURE

>> **KRAFT KITCHENS TIPS**
Buy ground beef in bulk and
freeze the excess, flattened,
in a sealable plastic freezer
bag — it will thaw more
quickly when you are ready
to use it.

Form individual hamburger
patties and freeze them,
layered, between pieces of
waxed paper, so they'll be
easy to separate without
thawing when you go to
use them.

Be sure to thoroughly wash
alfalfa sprouts before using.

MIX 1 lb ground meat with 1 egg and 1/4 to 1/2 cup crumbs. Shape into 4 patties, grill and serve on buns.

Master Burger Mixture is terrific in the following ways:

ISLAND BURGER
TOP a grilled burger made of ground pork with a pineapple ring and some sliced green onion. Serve on an onion bun.

CALIFORNIA BURGER
TOP a chicken burger with alfalfa sprouts and guacamole. Serve on a hamburger bun.

TACO BURGER
TOP a beef burger with lettuce, sliced tomato, salsa, guacamole and sour cream. Wrap into a large flour tortilla.

>> **TRY THIS, TOO** An ice-cream scoop easily portions out meat mixture when you make hamburger patties. If you're cooking for small children, scale down the burger patties to fit into tender dinner rolls.

California Burger

Burger Know-How

>> **KRAFT KITCHENS TIP**
If you're cooking hamburgers on the grill, resist the temptation to press down on them with your spatula. Those tidy pushes actually squeeze out the delicious juices at the center of the meat that make your burger moist and tender.

MEAT

Ground beef is by far the meat most commonly used for hamburgers. But why not try something a little different? Ground chicken, veal, turkey and pork also make terrific burgers.

CRUMBS

The amount of crumbs you will require depends on the type of meat you use. Softer meats, such as chicken, turkey and veal, will need more crumbs to help the burgers hold their shape. Start with 1/4 cup and gradually add more until you have a meat mixture that is not too sticky and is gathered easily into a ball.

Different folks prefer different kinds of crumbs. At the Kraft Kitchens, Susanne likes to used crushed crackers, Cayla opts for rolled oats, Lorna runs some tortilla chips through the food processor and Michele relies on good old-fashioned bread crumbs. All of them do the trick when it comes to helping hold that hamburger together.

BUNS

The classic hamburger bun is a great place to start, but slices of sourdough bread, large flour tortillas, pita pockets and onion buns also make interesting and tasty holders for your burger.

SAUSAGE KEBABS ON A BUN

Just follow our 3 simple steps:

1 CUT 4 Italian-style sausages into 2-inch pieces, cut 1 pepper into large chunks and a red onion into 8 wedges.

2 THREAD ingredients on 4 skewers and broil or grill them for 10 to 15 minutes, turning the skewers occasionally to brown evenly on all sides.

3 SET the skewers over 4 sliced buns, hold the ingredients in place with the buns and gently pull out the skewer. Serve with spicy ketchup, mustard or salsa.

MIX-AND-MATCH KIDS' PIZZAS

Just follow our 3 simple steps:

1 SPREAD pizza sauce on a prebaked pizza crust (1/4 cup should do it for a personal-sized pizza and 1 cup for a larger pizza crust).

2 TOP with **meat** (leftovers will do), a couple handfuls of shredded mozzarella, plus some Kraft 100% Grated Parmesan Cheese and some **toppings**.

3 BAKE at 450°F for 8 to 10 minutes or until the cheese is melted.

And use the ingredients you have on hand ...

>> KRAFT KITCHENS TIPS

Mix-and-Match Kids' Pizzas are a big hit at birthday parties, where everyone gets to design his or her own personal pizza.

If you don't have a pizza cutter, remember that kitchen scissors work just as well.

What **meat** do you feel like?	Finish with **toppings**
diced ham	pineapple
pepperoni	sliced mushrooms
bacon bits	sliced tomatoes
meatless	sliced mushrooms and tomatoes

ONE-PAN TACOS

>> KRAFT KITCHENS TIP
Toppings can be added at
the table to suit individual
tastes, which makes this
dish a real crowd pleaser.
We like to offer a varied
selection set out in
the cups of a muffin tin.

Just follow our 3 simple steps:

1 BROWN ground **meat** (1 lb should do it for 4) in a large nonstick skillet.

2 STIR in 2 cups *each* of Minute White Rice and water and 1 package
(1-1/4 oz) taco seasoning mix; bring contents to a boil.

3 SPRINKLE with Mexican-style shredded cheese, let stand for 5 minutes.
Top with tortilla chips, shredded lettuce, diced **veggies** and **topping**.

And use the ingredients you have on hand …

What **meat** do you feel like?	What **veggies** are on hand?	Now for the **topping**
chicken	tomatoes, peppers	salsa
beef	peppers, corn	sour cream
pork	tomatoes, onions	salsa
turkey	tomatoes, green onions	guacamole

Pork with Tomatoes and Onions

MIX-AND-MATCH DINNER PARCELS

Just follow our 3 simple steps:

1 MAKE a pouch, using a double thickness of foil.

2 SPOON 1/3 cup Minute White Rice, **meat** (1 piece per person should do it), a handful of sliced **veggies** and 1/3 cup **sauce** ingredients into the open mouth of your foil parcel, then double fold the opening to seal contents inside.

3 PLACE prepared parcel(s) on baking sheet and bake at 450°F for 15 minutes.

And use the ingredients you have on hand ...

>> KRAFT KITCHENS TIP
You can make parcels in advance, keep them in the refrigerator and bake as you need them – later the same day.

What **meat** do you feel like?	Now for the **veggies**	Try this **sauce**
chicken breast, sliced	carrots, green beans	chicken broth, dash of Italian seasoning
fish, cut into chunks	carrots, zucchini	Italian-style dressing
ham, diced	pineapple tidbits, peppers	pineapple juice
meatless	mushrooms, peppers, carrots, zucchini	vegetable broth

Chicken Breast with Carrots and Green Beans

15-MINUTE FAJITAS

>> **KRAFT KITCHENS TIP**
You can also use leftover grilled beef, chicken, pork or ham to make this delicious dish – in even less than 15 minutes.

Just follow our 3 simple steps:

1 STIR-FRY sliced **meat** (1 lb should do it for 4) with 2 tbsp **dressing** in a large nonstick skillet for 10 minutes.

2 ADD a couple handfuls of chopped **veggies** and cook 5 minutes more. Stir in 1/2 cup additional dressing to create a sauce.

3 SPOON filling into warmed flour tortillas and add your favorite toppings, such as lettuce, tomatoes and shredded cheese.

And use the ingredients you have on hand …

What **meat** do you feel like?	What **veggies** are on hand?	Now for the **dressing**
boneless chicken	onions, peppers, broccoli	Italian
beef sirloin	onions, mushrooms, tomatoes	ranch
ground beef	corn, tomatoes, green beans	Italian
meatless	onions, peppers, kidney beans	ranch

Chicken with Onions, Peppers and Broccoli

117

PULL-APART CALZONES

Just follow our 3 simple steps:

1 UNROLL 1 can (10 oz) refrigerated crescent dinner rolls and arrange on a large baking sheet. Spread surface with a couple spoonfuls of **sauce**.

2 TOP with a couple handfuls of chopped **meat/veggies** and **Kraft Shredded Cheese**. Unroll a second can of crescent rolls and arrange dough over top of the filling. Press edges together with fork, then cut rectangle into 4 triangles.

3 BAKE at 375°F for 17 minutes or until golden brown.

And use the ingredients you have on hand ...

What **meat/veggies** are on hand?	Try this **Kraft Shredded Cheese**	Now for the **sauce**
pepperoni	Italian Style	pizza or tomato sauce
ham	Cheddar	mayonnaise
cooked chicken	Mexican Style	salsa
mushrooms, green peppers and onions	mozzarella/Cheddar	ranch dressing

MAC-&-CHEESE PIZZA

Just follow our 3 simple steps:

1 PREPARE 1 package (7-1/4 oz) Kraft Macaroni & Cheese Dinner according to package directions; stir in 1 beaten egg.

2 PRESS the prepared macaroni and cheese onto a greased pie pan. Bake at 350°F for 5 minutes.

3 TOP with tomato sauce and your favorite pizza toppings, such as green peppers, mushrooms, pepperoni and shredded mozzarella cheese. Bake 15 minutes more or until heated through.

>> **SHARING OUR EXPERIENCES** This recipe combines two North American classics and right after we first thought of it — for a television commercial — it became an instant hit. Pizza is pizza everywhere, but our mac-and-cheese is known as Kraft Macaroni & Cheese Dinner in the U.S. and Kraft Dinner (or KD) in Canada. Either side of the border, it's also referred to affectionately as "the blue box." —Lorna, Kraft Kitchens

SPAGHETTI SQUASH PARMIGIANA BAKE

>> **KRAFT KITCHENS TIP**
Spaghetti squash is easy
to prepare and children
are always intrigued by
the fact that something
that looks very much like
spaghetti (and tastes
good, too) can come from
this plain, oddly shaped
vegetable. It's a very
appealing stand-in for
traditional pasta.

Just follow our 3 simple steps:

1 CUT 1 medium-sized spaghetti squash in half, lengthwise. Place one of the halves, cut-side down, in a microwavable dish; add 1/4 cup water. Microwave on HIGH for 7 minutes. Repeat with other half; scoop out cooked squash and place in a 9- x 13-inch baking dish.

2 MEANWHILE, brown 1 cup *each* of chopped onion, sliced mushrooms and chopped parsley in a spoonful or two of sun-dried tomato dressing. Add these cooked vegetables to the casserole dish and then mix in 1 can (28 oz) diced tomatoes. Finally, stir in 1 cup *each* of shredded mozzarella and grated Parmesan cheese.

3 TOP with additional cheese and bake at 400°F for 30 minutes.

CHEESE-AND-SPINACH CASSEROLE

DRAIN 2 packages (10 oz *each*) frozen spinach. (If you'd rather use fresh spinach, substitute 2 bunches for the package of frozen spinach.) Spread spinach in a shallow casserole, top with 1 cup cottage cheese and 1-1/2 cups *each* of shredded mozzarella cheese and Cheddar cheese. Sprinkle with 1 cup bread crumbs. Bake at 350°F for 15 to 20 minutes.

Spaghetti Squash Parmigiana Bake

SKY-HIGH VEGETABLE PIE

>> **KRAFT KITCHENS TIP**
Sky-High Vegetable Pie
is an excellent brunch dish,
and we think leftovers taste
better the second day than
they did the first.

1 package (6 oz) Stove Top Stuffing Mix, any flavor
5 eggs
1 cup shredded mozzarella cheese
1 package (10 oz) frozen chopped spinach, thawed and well drained
1 sliced red pepper
1 chopped onion
2 sliced tomatoes

1 PREPARE stuffing as directed on package. Lightly beat 1 egg and stir into the stuffing mixture. Press into greased 9-inch springform pan to form a crust.

2 SPRINKLE half the cheese over crust, evenly top with half the spinach, then add all the pepper and onion. Scatter remaining cheese and spinach over top, then beat 4 remaining eggs and pour over all.

3 TOP with tomato slices and bake at 400°F for 40 minutes or until the pie top is completely set. *Serves 4.*

EASY FALL RATATOUILLE

Just follow our 3 easy steps:
1 CUT 1 large eggplant into chunks. Cut 2 *each* onions, red peppers and zucchini into thick slices.
2 COOK vegetables in 1/2 cup sun-dried tomato dressing in a large non-stick skillet until tender and brown. Add 1 can (28 oz) whole tomatoes. Cook 15 minutes, allowing some of the juices to evaporate.
3 TOP with 1 cup *each* of grated Parmesan cheese and Italian-style shredded cheese. Cover and let stand 5 minutes or until the cheese is melted and the dish is heated through.

ZUCCHINI PUFFS

Just follow our 3 simple steps:
1 GRATE 3 medium zucchini (1-1/2 lb) into a large bowl.
2 MIX in 2 eggs, 1/4 cup flour, a spoonful of oil and 2 tsp thyme.
3 DROP by large spoonfuls into a nonstick skillet and cook at medium-high heat for about 3 minutes on each side or until the puffs are browned. Keep warm in a 200°F oven until you are ready to serve the entire batch. Serve with heated spaghetti sauce.

>> **KRAFT KITCHENS TIPS**
Buy eggplants that feel heavy for their size, are shiny in color and firm to the touch.

When shopping for zucchini, choose small zucchini, which will be younger, thinner skinned and more tender than the larger ones. Their skin should have a vibrant color and be free of blemishes.

15-MINUTE FLASH-IN-THE-PAN DINNERS

>> **KRAFT KITCHENS TIP**
Put water on the stove
as soon as you walk through
the door. While the pasta
cooks, you can take care
of preparing the ingredients
that will go with it.

Just follow our 3 simple steps:

1 COOK chopped onion in your choice of **dressing** in a nonstick skillet over medium heat.

2 CHOP remaining **veggies**, adding to the cooked onion a handful of the longest-cooking ones first. (See "Fast, Faster, Fastest" on page 4.)

3 SEASON with a bit more of your favorite dressing and sprinkle with a handful of **cheese** over top. Serve over your favorite pasta, rice or noodles.

And use the ingredients you have on hand ...

What **veggies** do you feel like?	Now for the **dressing**	Top with **cheese**
broccoli, peppers, mushrooms	Greek	crumbled feta
eggplant, tomatoes, zucchini	sun-dried tomato	shredded Italian-style
carrots, green beans, mushrooms	Italian	shredded Cheddar
cauliflower, tomatoes, spinach	balsamic	shredded Italian-style

Cauliflower, Tomatoes and Spinach

MAIN-DISH FRUIT-AND-CHEESE SALADS

Just follow our 3 simple steps:

1 PLACE washed salad greens, such as romaine, spinach or leaf lettuce, on plates.

2 ARRANGE sliced **fruit** and **cheese** over top.

3 DRIZZLE with **dressing**.

And use the ingredients you have on hand …

>> TRY THIS, TOO

Serve these salads with our warm 4-Ingredient Biscuits (page 147).

What **fruit** do you feel like?	What **cheese** is on hand?	Now for the **dressing**
pineapple	Havarti	Thousand Island
red and green Bartlett pears	Cheddar	peppercorn ranch
orange segments and red grapes	Gouda	French
green and red apples	mozzarella	raspberry vinaigrette

Red and Green Bartlett Pears with Cheddar

SIMPLE SIZZLING SALADS

>> **KRAFT KITCHENS TIP**
Make your own croutons
simply by baking cubed
bread on a baking sheet
in a 400°F oven for about
5 minutes.

Just follow our 3 simple steps:

1 STIR-FRY sliced **meat** (1 lb should do it for 4) with a spoonful of **Kraft Dressing** in a skillet for 10 minutes.

2 ADD sliced **veggies** (a handful per person) and cook 10 minutes more. Add an additional 1/2 cup dressing to make a sauce.

3 TOSS cooked meat and veggies with your favorite greens and a handful of homemade croutons (see our kitchen tip). Serve immediately.

And use the ingredients you have on hand …

What **meat** do you feel like?	What **veggies** are on hand?	Try this **Kraft Dressing**
boneless, skinless chicken	peppers	sun-dried tomato
sirloin steak	carrots	Italian
boneless pork	red onions	Catalina
meatless	peppers, onions, zucchini	balsamic vinaigrette

Sirloin-Steak-and-Carrot Sizzling Salad

CHICKEN TACO RANCH SALAD

TOSS 7 cups fresh salad greens with 1 cup sliced grilled chicken breast in a large bowl. Add a handful of shredded Cheddar cheese. Serve salad with ranch dressing, salsa and coarsely broken tortilla chips.

>> TRY THIS, TOO Serve this flavorful salad with our Southern-Style Cornbread (page 79). Orange sections sprinkled with cinnamon make a refreshing dessert.

>> KRAFT KITCHENS TIP A reminder to wash hands – and all kitchen utensils – in hot, soapy water after every contact with raw chicken.

Every family has dinnertime favorites. For the family cook, though, there are two sides to the situation. On the one hand, you know that every time you set those favorites on the table they're sure to be enjoyed. On the other hand, there are times when you'd just love to give such old familiars a little zip, an interesting twist to liven up the meal. And that's where the recipes in this section will come

Sides & Salads

in handy. Make your classic casseroles and skillet dishes new and exciting all over again with one of these easy, tasty sides or salads; vary your best-loved recipes with terrific seasonal ingredients – we'll show you how. With our take on homey and hearty vegetables, fresh salads, quick rolls and breads, you'll never run short of simple, interesting ways to give family favorites new appeal. And always the focus is on handy ingredients and quick-and-easy preparation. Just turn the page – we'll tell you how to make more great vegetarian dishes, too.

A Host of Vegetables 135

Biscuits and Breads 147

Rice and Stuffings 152

Salads and Greens 154

TOMATOES AND ZUCCHINI AU GRATIN

Just follow our 3 simple steps:

1 PLACE 2 tomatoes, halved, and 2 small zucchini, halved lengthwise, in a 9- x 13-inch baking dish.

2 MIX equal parts of shredded Swiss cheese and dry bread crumbs with a few spoonfuls of butter; scatter the mixture over your vegetables.

3 BAKE at 400°F for 8 to 10 minutes or until the cheese mixture is a light golden brown.

CREAMY CAULIFLOWER MEDLEY

Just follow our 2 simple steps:

1 COMBINE 1 diced onion, 1 medium cauliflower cut into florets, 1/2 red pepper, diced, and 1/2 cup *each* water and frozen green peas in a microwavable bowl, placing the diced onion on the bottom. Cover and microwave on HIGH for 9 to 10 minutes; drain.

2 MIX 1/3 cup *each* Miracle Whip, grated Parmesan cheese and sour cream. Toss mixture with cooked vegetables.

>> KRAFT KITCHENS TIPS
If you're cooking frozen vegetables, try sautéing them in a bit of Italian salad dressing as a flavorful change from simmering them in water.

To ripen a tomato quickly, place it in a paper bag or a covered bowl along with an apple. The apple gives off ethylene gas, which speeds up the ripening process for the tomato.

GLAZED CARROTS

>> KRAFT KITCHENS TIPS
To make Glazed Carrots a little more special, add 1 cup halved seedless green grapes as you stir in the butter.

Slice carrots on an angle for fast, even cooking. A light rinse is all that's necessary with young carrots, but older carrots should be peeled.

Just follow our 3 simple steps:
1 SLICE 8 medium carrots and place in a skillet with some water and 1 or 2 spoonfuls of orange marmalade.
2 COOK for a few minutes, until liquid evaporates and carrots are tender.
3 ADD a spoonful of butter and stir to mix with sauce.

PARMESAN CARROTS

Just follow our 3 simple steps:
1 STEAM 8 medium carrots, peeled and sliced in half lengthwise, until tender-crisp; drain.
2 BRUSH cooked carrots with melted butter and place in a shallow baking pan; sprinkle with a few spoonfuls of grated Parmesan cheese.
3 BROIL for 3 to 5 minutes or until cheese is golden; serve immediately.

ZUCCHINI AND CARROTS

Just follow our 3 simple steps:
1 SLICE 8 medium carrots. Place in saucepan with 1 cup water; cover. Cook on medium heat 10 minutes or until almost tender.
2 ADD 2 sliced zucchini and cook, covered, 6 minutes more. Drain.
3 ADD a spoonful of butter and a dash of dried marjoram; toss lightly.

Zucchini and Carrots, Parmesan Carrots

STALK-OF-THE-TOWN STIR-FRY

Just follow our 3 simple steps:
1 PEEL 3 broccoli stalks, then cut each stalk into several strips.
2 STIR-FRY in a skillet in 1 or 2 spoonfuls *each* of oil and soy sauce, adding a sliced red pepper after 1 minute.
3 TOP with 2 sliced green onions and serve immediately.

MIRACLE BROCCOLI BAKE

Just follow our 3 simple steps:
1 COOK 1 bunch chopped broccoli in simmering water or 2 packages (10 oz *each*) frozen broccoli spears according to package directions; drain well. Place cooked broccoli in a greased 9- x 13-inch baking dish. Sprinkle with 1 cup shredded Cheddar cheese and set aside.
2 MIX 2 eggs with 1 cup Miracle Whip, 1 can (10-3/4 oz) condensed cream of mushroom soup and 1/2 chopped onion; spread mixture over cheese and sprinkle top with bread crumbs.
3 BAKE at 350°F for 30 minutes or until heated through.

>> TRY THIS, TOO
For a tasty topping just right with steamed broccoli, microwave 1 cup Cheez Whiz on HIGH for 1 to 1-1/2 minutes, stirring until smooth and heated through. Stir in a handful of bacon bits, a dash of curry powder or a handful of chopped toasted pecans.

TRICOLOR GREEN BEAN SALUTE

>> KRAFT KITCHENS TIP
When buying green beans, choose slender, crisp beans that are bright in color and free of brown spots. You can substitute frozen beans for fresh beans in these recipes, if you like.

STIR-FRY 1 lb green beans with 1 *each* red pepper and yellow pepper, cut into strips, 1/2 sliced onion and 2 minced garlic cloves in 1 or 2 spoonfuls of zesty Italian dressing for 6 to 8 minutes or until the vegetables are tender-crisp. Season to taste and serve immediately.

CHEESE-AND-GARLIC GREEN BEANS

Just follow our 2 simple steps:
1 PLACE 3 cups green and yellow waxed beans, cut into 1-inch pieces, 1 minced garlic clove and 1/4 cup water in a microwavable bowl. Cover and cook on HIGH for 7 to 8 minutes or until the beans are tender; drain.
2 TOSS with a spoonful of butter and some grated Parmesan cheese.

GREEN BEANS AND TOMATOES ITALIANO

Just follow our 2 simple steps:
1 PLACE 3 cups green beans, 2 plum tomatoes cut into wedges and 1/4 cup sun-dried tomato dressing in a microwavable bowl; cover.
2 MICROWAVE on HIGH for 2 to 3 minutes or until vegetables are heated through, stirring them once. Sprinkle with a bit of fresh basil and serve immediately.

TEX-MEX SALSA SPUDS

Just follow our 3 simple steps:

1 PIERCE 2 baking potatoes with a fork in several places; then microwave on HIGH until they are tender, turning over at the halfway mark. (Large potatoes may take up to 10 minutes.)

2 CUT each potato in half, lengthwise; scoop out centers, leaving shells 1/4-inch thick. Mash scooped potato with 1/4 cup *each* of ranch dressing, sliced green onion and Kraft Mexican Style Shredded Cheese. Fill potato shells with the mixture.

3 TOP each filled potato half with a spoonful of mixed chopped pepper, green onion and cilantro. Sprinkle with additional shredded cheese. Bake at 375°F for 15 minutes or until potatoes are heated through.

>> **KRAFT KITCHENS TIP**
What is the best way to store potatoes at home? Many people make the mistake of storing potatoes in a plastic bag, which can accelerate decay. Instead, potatoes should be stored in a dark, cool, dry and well-ventilated space. (If left in direct light, potatoes will turn green.)

POTATO WEDGES AND PEPPERS

Just follow our 3 simple steps:

1 PLACE 3 large baking potatoes, cut into wedges, and 2 chopped peppers in a casserole pan.

2 POUR 1/2 cup sun-dried tomato dressing over top and cover pan with foil.

3 BAKE at 400°F for 45 minutes, then remove foil and bake 15 minutes more or until vegetables are tender and top surface has turned golden.

15-MINUTE MASHED SIDES

>> TRY THIS, TOO

For Philly Mashed Potatoes, simmer 6 potatoes until cooked and tender; drain and mash. Stir in 1/2 a tub (8 oz) Philadelphia Chive & Onion Cream Cheese Spread and serve immediately.

Just follow our 2 simple steps:

1 COOK chopped **veggies** (1 cup per person should do it) and **fruit** in simmering water until tender. Drain. Add a spoonful of butter to the pot and mash.

2 STIR in 1/2 cup Kraft Mayo and a dash of **add-ins**.

And use the ingredients you have on hand …

15-Minute Mashed Carrots

What **veggies** are on hand?	Add this **fruit**	Try these **add-ins**
turnip	apple	allspice
sweet potato	banana	ginger
potato	pear	nutmeg
carrot	1/2 cup crushed pineapple	cinnamon

4-INGREDIENT BISCUITS

Just follow our 3 simple steps:

1 MIX 2 cups flour with 1 tbsp baking powder. Cut in 1 tub (8 oz) of any flavor of Philadelphia Cream Cheese Spread to form a crumbly mixture. (Plain, herb-and-garlic and pineapple cream cheese are all great in this easy recipe.)

2 POUR 1/2 cup milk and a handful of add-ins into the cream cheese/flour mixture. (Some excellent add-ins to try are shredded Cheddar cheese, dried cranberries, grated orange or lemon peel and raisins.) Stir until dough holds together. On a floured surface, pat dough to a thickness of 3/4 inch. Using the top of a glass or a round or square cookie cutter, cut out 10 to 12 biscuits. Place on a cookie sheet.

3 BAKE at 425°F for 12 to 15 minutes.

>> **TRY THIS, TOO** This recipe makes terrific dumplings. Just drop the batter by spoonfuls into soup or stew and simmer for 10 to 15 minutes.

>> **KRAFT KITCHENS TIPS**
In this recipe, you can pour in all the milk at once and just mix briefly. Don't worry if small bits of cream cheese remain unblended.

Freeze cooled biscuits in a plastic bag or wrapped individually in plastic wrap for up to 1 month.

HOT CHEESE LOAF

>> KRAFT KITCHENS TIP
Change the taste and
the look of our Hot Cheese
Loaf by varying the
cheese you use. Try Swiss,
mozzarella or extra-sharp
Cheddar, for example.

Just follow our 3 simple steps:

1 MAKE about 10 cuts, 1 inch apart, into a loaf of French bread, cutting almost but not completely through the loaf each time. Brush with sun-dried tomato dressing on each cut side.

2 CUT approximately 5 slices of process cheese diagonally, to make 2 triangles per slice. Place 1 triangle in each cut and scatter with a bit of minced fresh basil.

3 WRAP the filled loaf in heavy-duty aluminum foil and bake at 350°F for 10 to 15 minutes or until process cheese has melted. Unwrap and serve immediately.

PARMESAN BREAD STICKS

Just follow our 3 simple steps:

1 SEPARATE 1 can (11 oz) refrigerated soft bread-stick dough into individual portions; cut each portion in half to make 16 pieces. Twist bread-stick pieces into shape and place on ungreased baking sheet.

2 BRUSH bread sticks with a little melted butter and sprinkle with grated Parmesan cheese.

3 PRESS the ends of each piece into place gently on the baking sheet to keep them from shrinking as they bake. Bake at 350°F for 14 to 18 minutes or until the bread sticks are golden brown.

TOMATO CHEESE BREAD

Just follow our 3 simple steps:

1 MAKE 12 wedge-shaped cuts into 1 round sourdough loaf, cutting almost but not completely through the loaf each time.

2 MIX 1 cup Kraft Mayo with 1/2 cup *each* of shredded mozzarella and grated Parmesan cheese. Stir in a handful *each* of chopped pitted black olives and chopped sun-dried tomatoes, mixing together thoroughly.

3 SPREAD cheese mixture into spaces between wedges of bread, then place prepared loaf on a baking sheet. Bake at 400°F for 10 minutes or until filling is completely melted. Sprinkle additional cheese over top and return loaf to oven, just until cheese has melted; serve immediately.

MIRACLE GARLIC BREAD 4 WAYS

Just follow our 3 simple steps:
1 MIX 1 cup Miracle Whip with 1/2 cup *each* of shredded mozzarella and grated Parmesan cheese.
2 ADD 1 minced garlic clove to the mixture and stir together well.
3 SPREAD evenly over toasted slices of French bread. Bake at 350°F for 5 to 7 minutes or until cheese has melted. Serve immediately.

Miracle Garlic Bread is terrific in the following ways:

BACON AND ONION
ADD a handful of bacon bits and 2 chopped green onions to the basic cheese mixture. Spread on slices of toasted pumpernickel and bake, as above.

EXTRA CHEESY
REPLACE the shredded mozzarella with an Italian-style shredded cheese. Spread the mixture on slices of toasted rye bread and bake, as above.

BETTA BRUSCHETTA
ADD a spoonful *each* of chopped tomato and diced red onion to the basic mixture, spread on toasted Kaiser rolls cut in half and bake, as above.

GREAT TAKES ON MINUTE RICE

>> **KRAFT KITCHENS TIP**
With Minute White Rice, you don't need to use the stove. You can microwave it, for example. (See package for directions.) You can also make it in a heatproof bowl. Just measure out your rice, add boiling water according to package directions and cover. Let stand for 5 minutes or until water is fully absorbed.

Prepare Minute White Rice according to package directions, substituting one of the following liquids. And always remember: equal amounts of liquid and Minute Rice.

BROTH Bring 1 can (10-3/4 oz) *each* of condensed broth-based soup and water to a boil. Stir in 2 matching cans of Minute White Rice, cover, remove from heat and let stand 5 minutes.

CREAM SOUP Bring 1 can (10-3/4 oz) *each* of condensed cream soup and water to a boil. Stir in 2 matching cans of Minute White Rice, cover, remove from heat and let stand 5 minutes.

PASTA SAUCE Bring 1 cup *each* of pasta sauce and water to a boil. Stir in 2 cups Minute White Rice, cover, remove from heat and let stand 5 minutes.

JUICE Substitute tomato, orange or apple juice for the quantity of water specified in the Minute White Rice package directions.

CANNED TOMATOES Bring 1 can *each* of chopped canned tomatoes and water to a boil. Stir in 2 matching cans Minute White Rice, cover, remove from heat and let stand 5 minutes.

And try these stir-ins in plain Minute White Rice:
> Fresh chopped fruit
> Dried fruits, including raisins and chopped apricot
> Fresh herbs, such as parsley and basil
> Shredded cheese or grated Parmesan cheese
> Grated orange or lemon peel

STUFFINGS SIMPLIFIED

APPLE STUFFING
1 PREPARE 1 package Stove Top Stuffing Mix for turkey, by mixing contents of the vegetable/seasoning package with 1 cup apple juice.
2 ADD 2 tbsp butter. Bring to a boil. Reduce heat, cover and simmer for 5 minutes.
3 STIR in 1 chopped apple and the stuffing crumbs. Cover, remove from heat and let stand 5 minutes. Serve immediately.

CHEESE STUFFING
1 PREPARE 1 package Stove Top Stuffing Mix, chicken flavor, by mixing contents of vegetable/seasoning package with 1 cup water.
2 ADD 2 tbsp butter or margarine and 1 chopped zucchini. Bring to a boil, reduce heat, cover and simmer for 5 minutes.
3 STIR in 1 cup shredded Cheddar cheese and stuffing crumbs. Cover, remove from heat and let stand 5 minutes. Serve immediately.

BACON-AND-MUSHROOM STUFFING
1 PREPARE 1 package Stove Top Stuffing Mix, your favorite flavor, according to package directions.
2 STIR in a handful of cooked and crumbled bacon and 1 cup *each* chopped cooked mushrooms and onions at the end of the cooking time. Cover, remove from heat and let stand 5 minutes.

>> **SHARING OUR EXPERIENCES**
Whenever I have leftover chicken, I make a box of stuffing so my family can have chicken-and-stuffing sandwiches for lunch.
—Susanne, Kraft Kitchens

SHREDDED TOSTADA SALAD

>> KRAFT KITCHEN TIPS
To prepare iceberg lettuce, loosen the core by hitting the stem end sharply on the counter. Twist the core and lift out. To remove excess moisture, wrap the lettuce in a clean kitchen towel or several layers of paper towel.

A medium-sized head of iceberg lettuce will provide about 10 cups of lettuce.

Just follow our 2 simple steps:
1 SHRED half a head of iceberg lettuce and mix with a few spoonfuls *each* of chopped red pepper, corn and black beans (drained and rinsed) in a large serving bowl. Add a couple of handfuls *each* of Kraft Mexican Style Shredded Cheese and crushed nacho chips.
2 TOSS with sun-dried tomato dressing, sprinkle a few extra crumbled nacho chips over top and serve.

CHOPPED BLT SALAD

Just follow our 3 simple steps:
1 CHOP half a head of iceberg lettuce and line a platter with the pieces.
2 ARRANGE in rows on top of the lettuce a handful of bacon bits, a handful *each* of peas or cubed avocado, chopped tomato, shredded Cheddar cheese and croutons.
3 DRIZZLE with a creamy cucumber or ranch dressing.

CLASSIC TORN GREEK SALAD

Just follow our 2 simple steps:
1 TEAR half a head of iceberg lettuce and combine with a handful *each* of black olives, crumbled feta cheese, chopped tomato, cucumber and red onion.
2 TOSS with a Greek vinaigrette dressing and serve with toasted pita wedges.

SO MANY COLESLAWS

Just follow our 2 simple steps:

1 COMBINE 1/2 head of shredded **cabbage** with **add-ins** in a large bowl.

2 TOSS with 1/2 cup **Kraft Dressing**.

And use the ingredients you have on hand …

>> **KRAFT KITCHENS TIP**
A small head of cabbage will give you about 8 cups of shredded cabbage. It will keep in the refrigerator for up to 6 days.

Start with this **cabbage**	Stir in these **add-ins**	Pour on this **Kraft Dressing**
green	1 <u>each</u> chopped zucchini and apple, plus 1/2 sliced red onion	ranch
red	2 shredded carrots, 1 sliced green onion and handfuls of parsley and raisins	coleslaw
Nappa	1/2 sliced red onion and 1 can (10 oz) drained mandarin orange segments	Catalina
red and green	1 cup <u>each</u> chopped cauliflower and broccoli, plus a handful of raisins	zesty Italian

Green Cabbage with Zucchini and Apple

TANGY BROCCOLI SALAD

>> **KRAFT KITCHENS TIP**
To further save time, you can purchase cut-up broccoli florets from your grocer's salad bar or produce section.

Just follow our 2 simple steps:
1 MIX 1 cup Miracle Whip with 2 tbsp *each* of sugar and vinegar in a large serving bowl.
2 ADD 1 medium-sized bunch of broccoli cut into florets, a handful of bacon bits and 1/2 chopped red onion. Refrigerate until ready to serve.

HEADS-UP RANCH SALAD

Just follow our 3 simple steps:
1 MIX 1 large bunch of broccoli cut into florets, 1 carrot cut into sticks, and 1/2 cup *each* of chopped red onion and raisins.
2 POUR 1/2 cup ranch dressing over salad and toss lightly.
3 REFRIGERATE until ready to serve.

Tangy Broccoli Salad

Perfect Partners for Your Greens

ARUGULA (ROCKET, RUGULA)
keeps for up to 4 days

Tender, dark green leaves with pungent flavor to combine with subtler greens.
Combine in salads with Boston, leaf, romaine or iceberg lettuce or radicchio.
GOES WITH *a balsamic or creamy cucumber dressing.*

BELGIAN ENDIVE
keeps for up to 7 days

Pale yellow leaves on a cream-colored stalk with a delicately bitter crunch.
Combine in salads with Boston lettuce, watercress, arugula or radicchio.
GOES WITH *a blue cheese or ranch dressing.*

BOSTON (BIBB)
keeps for 1–2 days

A loosely packed head with soft-textured tender leaves. Mild buttery flavor.
Combine in salads with leaf lettuce or spinach.
GOES WITH *light and creamy dressings.*

ICEBERG
keeps for up to 7 days

This popular lettuce heightens the flavors of other greens. Adds a crisp texture.
Combine in salads with arugula, watercress or leaf lettuce.
GOES WITH *Kraft Catalina or Thousand Island dressing.*

LEAF LETTUCE
keeps for 2–3 days

Sprawling ruffled delicate leaves with mild flavor. Dress just prior to serving.
Combine in salads with Boston or iceberg lettuce, radicchio or arugula.
GOES WITH *Italian or herb dressing.*

MESCLUN
keeps for 2–3 days

Mix may include arugula, chervil, frisée, dandelion greens and lamb's lettuce. Great on its own or in combination with radicchio or any leaf lettuce.

GOES WITH *herb or garlic dressing.*

RADICCHIO
keeps for up to 14 days

Tight head of tiny maroon leaves with a delicately peppery, chewy crunch. Combine in salads with Boston or leaf lettuce, spinach or Belgian endive.

GOES WITH *sun-dried tomato or balsamic dressing.*

ROMAINE
keeps for up to 7 days

Large, sweet-tasting, succulent crisp leaves. The foundation of Caesar salads. Combine in salads with spinach, arugula or watercress.

GOES WITH *Caesar or creamy Italian dressing.*

SPINACH
keeps for 3–4 days

Sturdy nutrient-rich tart leaves. Soak in cold water and rinse to remove sand. Combine in salads with radicchio, romaine, Boston or leaf lettuce.

GOES WITH *tomato-based or French dressing.*

WATERCRESS
keeps for 3–4 days

Tender round dark green leaves on thin, crisp stems with spicy, peppery flavor. Combine in salads with romaine, Boston or iceberg lettuce.

GOES WITH *light and creamy dressings.*

Weeknight desserts don't have to be fancy to be just fine. We know that at the end of a busy day what you want is a dessert that's simple and sweet, an easy treat for everyone. That last little bit of indulgence that gives you and your family an extra reason to linger a few minutes longer around the table. In this section, you'll find all sorts of great suggestions for terrific family-pleasing

Desserts

desserts you can pull together in just a few minutes' time. Desserts with genuine home-made appeal. Turn the page to find a wide range of sweet treats to please the chocolate lover or satisfy a craving for the taste of fruit. Cool and creamy delights. Or perhaps something right out of the oven, warmly scented with cinnamon and sugar. And, of course, all kinds of desserts just right for the youngest members of the family. Whatever your taste for dessert tonight, in this section of Dinner on Hand you'll find sweet ideas just perfect for your family.

Spoon Sweets   165
Simple Home Baking   173
Fruit as a Finish   178
Cookie Inspirations   181
Ice Cream Plus   183

MIX-IT-UP PUDDINGS

Just follow our 3 simple steps:

1 PREPARE 1 package (4-serving size) **Jell-O Instant Pudding** according to package directions.

2 SPOON into individual serving dishes.

3 TOP with your favorite **topping**.

And use the ingredients you have on hand ...

>> KRAFT KITCHENS TIPS

Enjoy one-bowl instant pudding in 5 minutes. Just pour milk and pudding mix into a 1 qt container, cover with an airtight lid and shake until pudding thickens – there's no need to use a hand mixer here.

Watching your calories? Substitute light instant pudding instead.

What **Jell-O Instant Pudding** do you feel like?	Try these **toppings**
vanilla	fresh or canned sliced or chopped fruit
pistachio	miniature marshmallows
chocolate	small pieces of sandwich cookies
butterscotch	sliced banana and chopped nuts

SO MANY QUICK DESSERTS

>> KRAFT KITCHENS TIP
These frozen add-ins instantly chill the gelatin, so the dessert is set by the time you finish dinner.

Just follow our 3 simple steps:

1 DISSOLVE 1 package (4-serving size) **Jell-O Gelatin** in 1 cup boiling water.

2 WHISK in 2 cups of **add-ins** and a few handfuls of **extras**.

3 POUR into 4 individual dessert dishes; chill until set. Top with more extras, if you like.

And use the ingredients you have on hand …

What **Jell-O Gelatin** do you feel like?	Try these **add-ins**	Now the **extras**
orange	vanilla ice cream	chocolate chips
strawberry	frozen strawberries	sliced almonds
lemon	frozen strawberry yogurt	drained mandarin segments
raspberry	frozen raspberry sorbet	grated orange peel

Orange Quick Dessert

EVERYTHING IN A CLOUD

FRUIT IN A CLOUD

Just follow our 2 simple steps:
1 SPOON a generous dollop of Cool Whip into an individual dessert dish. Using back of spoon, make depression in center, spreading whipped topping up sides of dish. Refrigerate until ready to serve.
2 FILL whipped topping "cup" with assorted fresh or canned fruit.

PUDDING IN A CLOUD

Just follow our 2 simple steps:
1 SPOON a generous dollop of Cool Whip into an individual dessert dish. Using back of spoon, make depression in center, spreading whipped topping up sides of dish.
2 FILL whipped topping "cup" with prepared instant chocolate pudding. Refrigerate until ready to serve.

CUBES IN A CLOUD

Just follow our 2 simple steps:
1 SPOON a generous dollop of Cool Whip into an individual dessert dish. Using back of spoon, make depression in center, spreading whipped topping up sides of dish.
2 FILL whipped topping "cup" with cubes of fruit gelatin, your favorite flavor. Refrigerate until ready to serve.

ROCKY ROAD CUPS

Just follow our 2 simple steps:

1 STIR a handful of miniature marshmallows and semisweet chocolate chips into a Jell-O Chocolate Pudding Snack.

2 MICROWAVE on HIGH for 20 seconds, just until the chocolate chips and marshmallows begin to melt. Serve warm.

TROPICAL DELIGHT

Just follow our 3 simple steps:

1 MIX 1 package (4-serving size) Jell-O Vanilla Instant Pudding & Pie Filling with 1 can (19 oz) crushed pineapple, including juice, in a bowl.

2 ADD 1 can (10 oz) drained mandarin orange segments and 1 sliced banana.

3 SPOON into 6 serving dishes; chill 5 minutes. Top with toasted coconut.

DIRT CUPS

Just follow our 3 simple steps:

1 PREPARE 1 package (4-serving size) Jell-O Chocolate Instant Pudding according to package directions.

2 FOLD in 2 cups whipped topping and 1/2 cup chocolate wafer crumbs.

3 TO assemble, place a spoonful of crushed wafer crumbs in the bottom of 6 dessert dishes. Fill each dish three-quarters full with pudding mixture. Top with additional cookie crumbs and garnish with gummy worms. Chill.

EVERYDAY EASY BROWNIES

Just follow our 3 simple steps:

1 PARTIALLY melt 4 squares of chopped Baker's Unsweetened Baking Chocolate with 3/4 cup butter in microwave on MED for 3 minutes. Stir until butter and chocolate are completely melted.

2 ADD 3 eggs and stir until well blended. Stir in 1-1/2 cups sugar, 1 cup all-purpose flour and 1 cup chopped nuts (optional).

3 SPREAD in a greased 9- x 13-inch pan. Bake at 350°F for 30 minutes.

Everyday Easy Brownies are terrific in the following ways:

CREAM CHEESE SWIRL

COMBINE 1 package (8 oz) softened cream cheese with 1/4 cup sugar, stirring together until mixture is completely smooth. Mix in 1 egg and 2 spoonfuls of raspberry jam, stirring well. Drop spoonfuls of mixture over brownie batter, swirl together with a knife to create a marbled effect and bake as directed.

ROCKY ROAD

TOP brownies with chopped semisweet chocolate and miniature marshmallows when they are nearly baked; return to oven for 5 minutes more.

PEANUT BUTTER SWIRL

DROP spoonfuls of peanut butter and 2 squares chopped semisweet chocolate over brownies while they are still warm. When peanut butter and chocolate melt, gently swirl a knife over them to create a marbled topping.

>> **KRAFT KITCHENS TIP**

To make a drizzled chocolate topping on your brownies, place 2 squares of chopped semisweet chocolate inside a sealable plastic bag and microwave on MED for 2-1/2 minutes or until chocolate has melted completely. Snip off one of the bottom corners of the bag and gently squeeze chocolate over cooled brownies.

ONE-BOWL BAKED GOODIES

>> KRAFT KITCHENS TIP
This recipe freezes well,
so you may want to bake a
double batch and freeze
half for unexpected guests.

Just follow our 3 simple steps:

1 BEAT together 4 eggs, 2 cups sugar and 1 cup Miracle Whip.

2 ADD 3 cups flour, 2 tsp baking soda, **fruit/veggies** and **add-ins**.

3 BAKE in a greased **pan** in a 350°F oven for the appropriate amount of time, according to the type of pan you are using.

And use the ingredients you have on hand …

Pineapple-Carrot Muffins

What **fruit/veggies** do you feel like?	Now for the **add-ins**	Bake in a **pan**
3 ripe mashed bananas	a handful of chopped nuts and a few dashes of ground nutmeg	2 loaf pans for 50 to 55 minutes
1 can drained pineapple tidbits and a handful of shredded carrot	a few dashes of ground allspice	2 muffin tins for 30 minutes
1-1/2 cups applesauce	a handful of raisins	9- x 13-inch pan for 45 to 50 minutes
a few spoonfuls of grated orange peel	1 cup orange juice and a few spoonfuls of poppy seeds	Bundt pan for 50 to 55 minutes

Banana Loaf

MIX-EASY CAKE

Just follow our 3 simple steps:

1 HEAT 1/3 cup oil and **chocolate** or **butterscotch** in an 8-inch square nonstick pan in a 350°F oven for 2 minutes. Stir with a fork until smooth.

2 ADD 3/4 cup *each* of **liquid** and sugar, 1 egg, 1-1/4 cups flour and 1/2 tsp baking soda. Stir together until smooth – about 2 minutes. Stir in a handful of **add-ins**, reserving some to scatter over top.

3 BAKE for 30 minutes or until a toothpick inserted comes out clean. Cool.

And use the ingredients you have on hand …

>> **KRAFT KITCHENS TIPS**
For easy cleanup, line pan with a double layer of foil.

No wooden toothpick? Use a piece of uncooked spaghetti instead.

What **chocolate** or **butterscotch** do you like?	Add the **liquid**	Try these **add-ins**
2 squares semisweet chocolate	coffee	shredded coconut and chopped pecans
2 squares unsweetened chocolate	water	chopped walnuts and semisweet chocolate chips
2 squares white chocolate	orange juice	chopped almonds and dried apricots, plus a spoonful of orange peel
1 cup butterscotch chips	water	chopped walnuts

PEANUT-BUTTER FRUIT DIP

>> **KRAFT KITCHENS TIPS**
Leftover Peanut-Butter
Fruit Dip can be stored in
the refrigerator and then
reheated in the microwave
just before using.

Another terrific instant
dessert idea? Melt peanut
butter in the microwave, then
drizzle it over ice cream,
along with chocolate sauce,
for a quick dessert.

Just follow our 2 simple steps:
1 MICROWAVE 1 cup peanut butter with 3 squares of white chocolate on MED for 2-1/2 minutes. Stir together until mixture is completely smooth.
2 STIR in a large spoonful of whipped topping. Serve with fresh fruit.

PINEAPPLE CREAM-CHEESE DIP

Just follow our 2 simple steps:
1 BLEND 1 tub (8 oz) Philadelphia Cream Cheese Spread with some pineapple juice until your dip is the desired consistency, then sweeten it with a little granulated or confectioners' sugar.
2 SERVE with assorted fruit, cut into pieces suitable for dipping.

>> **SHARING OUR EXPERIENCES** Dips such as these are great ways to get young children to eat fruit. We have found that the following choices work especially well: pineapple spears, pear and apple wedges, chunks or slices of banana and kiwi fruit, orange segments and whole strawberries.
—Lorna, Kraft Kitchens

COOKIE TREATS

Just follow our 2 simple steps:
1 SPREAD a spoonful of Cool Whip between chocolate wafer or chocolate chip cookies.
2 ROLL the edges of your cookie sandwiches in miniature chocolate chips or colored sprinkles. Serve immediately or store in an airtight container in the freezer.

CHOCOLATE-DIPPED GRAHAM CRACKERS

Just follow our 2 simple steps:
1 MELT 1 package (8 oz) chopped semisweet chocolate squares in a microwavable measuring cup on MED for 3 minutes. (NOTE: Chocolate will not be completely melted.) Stir until chocolate finishes melting and is smooth. Line a baking pan or cookie sheet with waxed paper.
2 DIP graham crackers into the melted chocolate, let the excess chocolate drip off, then set coated cracker pieces on the lined baking pan and chill before serving.

>> **KRAFT KITCHENS TIPS**
Chocolate can be partially melted in the microwave. For 2 squares of chocolate, heat on MED for 2 minutes – it's important that some chocolate remain unmelted. After microwaving, stir until chocolate is completely melted and smooth.

To melt more chocolate, increase microwave time by 30-second intervals for every 2 additional squares. Microwave ovens vary in efficiency, so take care not to overheat (and scorch) your chocolate.

COOKIES-AND-MILK AND MORE

>> **KRAFT KITCHENS TIPS**
Don't have any crumbs to
make a pie crust? Cookies
work just as well. Give
your favorite cookie a whirl
in the food processor or
blender and substitute
for prepared crumbs. Basic
crust recipe is 1-1/4 cups
prepared crumbs with
1/4 cup melted butter.

What's your favorite cookie partnership? Here are a few we really enjoy:

> Oreo chocolate sandwich cookies with milk, fruit juice, ice cream or a milkshake
> Ginger cookies with fresh fruit, sherbet or herbal tea
> Chocolate chip cookies with ice cream, a milkshake, milk or coffee
> Digestive cookies or graham crackers with cheese, fresh fruit, tea or coffee
> Oatmeal cookies with milk, fruit juice, tea or coffee

FRUIT-AND-SPICE ICE CREAM

Just follow our 2 simple steps:

1 SPOON vanilla ice cream into individual serving dishes.

2 TOP with sliced fresh or canned fruit such as oranges, bananas or pears, then sprinkle with a dash of ground cinnamon.

FROZEN BANANA POPS

Just follow our 2 simple steps:

1 FREEZE peeled bananas, wrapped individually in plastic wrap.

2 SERVE 1 per person, with a small bowl of chopped nuts for dipping.

FRUIT SPARKLE SAUCE

Just follow our 3 simple steps:

1 DRAIN 2 cans (19 oz *each*) fruit cocktail, reserving juice. Combine juice with 1/4 cup sugar, 2 tbsp cornstarch and 1/3 cup thawed orange juice concentrate in a microwavable bowl.

2 MICROWAVE on HIGH until fruit sauce comes to a boil, about 4 minutes. Microwave on MED for 3 minutes more, stirring several times.

3 STIR in fruit cocktail and serve warm over ice cream, pound cake or angel food cake.

>> **KRAFT KITCHEN TIPS**

Fruit Sparkle Sauce can be made ahead and stored in the refrigerator. Before serving, briefly reheat it in the microwave.

This sauce can also be made on the stove: Combine sauce ingredients in a saucepan, bring to a boil and then cook over medium heat for 3 to 5 minutes, stirring constantly.

Index

Almond Chicken, 69
Ants on a Log, 27
Apples
    Apple Stuffing, 153
    Cheese-and-Apple on Raisin Bread,
        100
Asian Know-How, 87
Asian Noodle Dinners, Easy, 88
Avocado Dip, 14

Bacon
    Bacon-and-Mushroom Stuffing, 153
    Bacon-and-Onion Miracle Garlic
        Bread, 151
Baked Goodies, One-Bowl, 174
Bananas
    Frozen Banana Pops, 183
    Peanut-Butter-and-Banana
        Smoothie, 24
Beef
ground:
    Cajun Dirty Rice, 75
    Cheesy Burritos, 83
    Everyday Easy Macaroni Dinners, 57
    15-Minute Fajitas, 116
    Last-Minute Monster Meatball
        Sandwich, 58
    Master Burger Mixture, 106

Master Meatballs Mixture, 58
Mix-and-Match Potato Dinners, 38
Muchos Tacos Master Mixture, 80
One-Pan Tacos, 112
One-Pot Saucy Pastas, 53
Pasta Bakes, 37
Saucy Meatball Supper, 58
roast:
    Hot-and-Cheesy Pull-Aparts, 105
    Warm Handheld Sandwiches, 95
sirloin:
    Easy Asian Noodle Dinners, 88
    15-Minute Fajitas, 116
    One-Pot Curry-and-Rice Dinners, 92
    Simple Sizzling Salads, 128
    Simple Stir-Fry, 47
Berry Crush, 24
Biscuits, 4-Ingredient, 147
Breads
    Hot Cheese Loaf, 148
    Miracle Garlic Bread 4 Ways, 151
    Parmesan Bread Sticks, 148
    Southern-Style Cornbread, 79
    Tomato Cheese Bread, 149
Broccoli, 18, 47, 158 (tips)
    Broccoli Dip, 14
    Cheesy Broccoli Soup, 50
    Heads-Up Ranch Salad, 158

Miracle Broccoli Bake, 139
Stalk-of-the-Town Stir-Fry, 139
Tangy Broccoli Salad, 158
Brownies, Everyday Easy, 173
Bruschetta, Betta, 151
Burgers, 106, 108 (tips)
    California Burger, 106
    Island Burger, 106
    Taco Burger, 106
Burritos, Cheesy, 83

Cabbage, 157 (tip)
    So Many Coleslaws, 157
Cajun Dirty Rice, 75
Cake, Mix-Easy, 177
Calzones, Pull-Apart, 118
Carrots, 18, 136 (tips)
    15-Minute Mashed Sides, 144
    Glazed Carrots, 136
    Parmesan Carrots, 136
    Zucchini and Carrots, 136
Casseroles and bakes
    Cheese-and-Spinach Casserole, 120
    Cheese Strata, 41
    Cheesy Burritos, 83
    Chili Bake, 31
    Everyday Easy Rice Dinners, 34
    Miracle Broccoli Bake, 139

Mix-and-Match Chicken Bakes, 66
Mix-and-Match Potato Dinners, 38
One-Pan Dinner Bakes, 62
Orange Pork Bake, 61
Oven-Tender Barbecue Bakes, 33
Pasta Bakes, 37
Spaghetti Squash Parmigiana Bake,
    120
Cauliflower Medley, Creamy, 135
Cheese, 21, 23, 38 (tips) *See also* Cream
cheese; Parmesan
    Cheese-and-Apple on Raisin Bread,
        100
    Cheese-and-Cracker Partners, 23
    Cheese-and-Garlic Green Beans,
        140
    Cheese-and-Spinach Casserole, 120
    Cheese-and-Vegetable Kebabs, 27
    Cheese Strata, 41
    Cheese Stuffing, 153
    Cheesy Broccoli Soup, 50
    Cheesy Burritos, 83
    Extra Cheesy Miracle Garlic Bread,
        151
    Grilled Cheese-and-Ham Monte
        Cristo, 100
    Grilled Cheese-and-Vegetable Pita,
        100

Hot-and-Cheesy Pull-Aparts, 105
Hot Cheese Loaf, 148
Main-Dish Fruit-and-Cheese Salads,
    127
Salsa Cheese Dip, 17
10 Ways with Grilled Cheese, 99
Tomato Cheese Bread, 149
Chicken, 64-65, 69, 131 (tips)
boneless:
    Cheesy Burritos, 83
    Chili Bake, 31
    Easy Asian Noodle Dinners, 88
    Everyday Easy Macaroni Dinners, 57
    Everyday Easy Rice Dinners, 34
    15-Minute Fajitas, 116
    Homemade Chicken Fingers, 71
    Master Crispy Chicken Coating, 68
    Mix-and-Match Potato Dinners, 38
    One-Pan Dinner Bakes, 62
    One-Pot Curry-and-Rice Dinners,
        92
    Oven-Tender Barbecue Bakes, 33
    Quick Paella, 84
    Simple Sizzling Salads, 128
breasts:
    Mix-and-Match Dinner Parcels, 115
    One-Pot Rice Dinners, 44
    Simple Stir-Fry, 47

cooked:
    Chicken Taco Ranch Salad, 131
    Easy Dinner Melts, 102
    Pull-Apart Calzones, 118
    Warm Handheld Sandwiches, 95
ground:
    California Burger, 106
    One-Pan Tacos, 112
pieces:
    Mix-and-Match Chicken Bakes, 66
    Oven-Tender Barbecue Bakes, 33
strips:
    One-Pot Saucy Pastas, 53
    Pasta Bakes, 37
wings:
    Shake 'N Bake Spicy Barbecue
        Wings, 71
Chickpea Dip, 14
Chili Bake, 31
Chocolate, 181 (tip)
    Chocolate-Dipped Graham
        Crackers, 181
    Cookie Treats, 181
    Dirt Cups, 170
    Everyday Easy Brownies, 173
    Mix-Easy Cake, 177
    Mix-It-Up Puddings, 165
    Pudding in a Cloud, 169

Rocky Road Cups, 170
Coconut-Curry Chicken, Crispy, 69
Collard Greens, Seasoned, 76
Cookies
    cookie-crumb pie crust, 182 (tip)
    Cookies-and-Milk and More, 182
    Cookie Treats, 181
Cornbread, Southern-Style, 79
Corn Chowder, Tex-Mex, 51
Cream cheese
    Philly Mashed Potatoes, 144
    Pineapple Cream-Cheese Dip, 178
Croutons, make-your-own, 128 (tip)
Cucumber Dip, 14
Curry, 92 (tip)
    Crispy Coconut-Curry Chicken, 69
    One-Pot Curry-and-Rice Dinners, 92

Desserts. *See also* Cookies; Ice cream; Puddings
    Chocolate-Dipped Graham Crackers, 181
    Dirt Cups, 170
    Everyday Easy Brownies, 173
    Everything in a Cloud, 169
    Frozen Banana Pops, 183
    One-Bowl Baked Goodies, 174

Peanut-Butter Fruit Dip, 178
Pineapple Cream Cheese Dip, 178
Rocky Road Cups, 170
So Many Quick Desserts, 166
Tropical Delight, 170
Dinnertime tips, 42-43
Dips
    Avocado Dip, 14
    Broccoli Dip, 14
    Chickpea Dip, 14
    Cool Dips, 17
    Cucumber Dip, 14
    Peanut-Butter Fruit Dip, 178
    Pineapple Cream-Cheese Dip, 178
    Quick Vegetable Dips, 14
    Salsa Cheese Dip, 17
    Spinach Dip, 14
    vegetables for, 17, 18-19 (tips)
Dirt Cups, 170

Eggplant, 123 (tip)
    Easy Fall Ratatouille, 123
Eggs, 41 (tip)
    Cheese Strata, 41
    Easy Dinner Melts, 102
Equipment, 6-7

Fajitas, 15-Minute, 116

Fish, 72 (tip)
    Mix-and-Match Dinner Parcels, 115
    Oven-Baked Fish and Chips, 72
    Saucy Microwave Fish Supper, 72
Fruit
    Fruit-and-Spice Ice Cream, 183
    Fruit in a Cloud, 169
    Fruit Sparkle Sauce, 183
    Fruity Shake, 24
    Main-Dish Fruit-and-Cheese Salads, 127
    Peanut-Butter Fruit Dip, 178

Garlic
    Cheese-and-Garlic Green Beans, 140
    Miracle Garlic Bread 4 Ways, 151
Green beans, 19, 140 (tips)
    Cheese-and-Garlic Green Beans, 140
    Green Beans and Tomatoes Italiano, 140
    Tricolor Green Bean Salute, 140
Greens, 160-61 (tips)

Ham
    Club on a Bun, 101
    Easy Asian Noodle Dinners, 88

Easy Dinner Melts, 102
Hot-and-Cheesy Pull-Aparts, 105
Meal-in-One Dinner Sandwiches, 96
Mix-and-Match Dinner Parcels, 115
Mix-and-Match Kids' Pizzas, 111
One-Pot Rice Dinners, 44
One-Pot Saucy Pastas, 53
Pull-Apart Calzones, 118
Quesadillas, 22
Quick Jambalaya, 75
Warm Handheld Sandwiches, 95

Ice cream
    Fruit-and-Spice Ice Cream, 183
    Fruit Sparkle Sauce, 183
    peanut-butter-and-chocolate sauce
        for, 178 (tip)

Jambalaya, Quick, 75
Jell-O
    Cubes in a Cloud, 169
    So Many Quick Desserts, 166

Kebabs
    Cheese-and-Vegetable Kebabs, 27
    Sausage Kebabs on a Bun, 109
Kids
    Ants on a Log, 27

Cheese-and-Vegetable Kebabs, 27
Cookie Treats, 181
Cubes in a Cloud, 169
Dirt Cups, 170
Double-Decker Tacos, 80
Everything in a Cloud, 169
15-Minute Nachos, 21
Frozen Banana Pops, 183
Mac & Cheese Pizza, 119
Meat-and-Cheese Dominoes, 27
Mexican Pizza Snack, 21
Mix-and-Match Kids' Pizzas, 111
Mix-It-Up Puddings, 165
No-Bake Munch Mix, 13
Peanut-Butter-and-Banana
    Smoothie, 24
Peanut-Butter-and-Banana Wrap, 27
Peanut-Butter Fruit Dip, 178
Popcorn Crunch, 13
Pudding in a Cloud, 169
Quesadillas, 22
Rocky Road Cups, 170
Shakes and Smoothies, 24
Snacktivities for Kids, 27
10 Ways with Grilled Cheese, 99
tips, 14, 27, 106, 178
tortilla cups, 80 (tip)
Kraft Kitchens hotline, 8

Lettuce, iceberg, 154, 160 (tips)
    Chopped BLT Salad, 154
    Classic Torn Greek Salad, 154
    Shredded Tostada Salad, 154

Macaroni
    Everyday Easy Macaroni Dinners, 57
    Mac & Cheese Pizza, 119
    Noodle Taco Bowls, 80
Meat-and-Cheese Dominoes, 27
Meatballs
    Last-Minute Monster Meatball
        Sandwich, 58
    Master Meatballs Mixture, 58
    Saucy Meatball Supper, 58
Meatless main dishes
    Cheese Strata, 41
    Cheesy Burritos, 83
    Easy Asian Noodle Dinners, 88
    Everyday Easy Macaroni Dinners, 57
    15-Minute Fajitas, 116
    15-Minute Flash-in-the-Pan Dinners,
        124
    Hot-and-Cheesy Pull-Aparts, 105
    Last-Minute Pastas, 54
    Meal-in-One Dinner Sandwiches, 96
    Mix-and-Match Dinner Parcels, 115
    Mix-and-Match Kids' Pizzas, 111

Mix-and-Match Potato Dinners, 38
One-Pan Dinner Bakes, 62
One-Pot Curry-and-Rice Dinners, 92
One-Pot Rice Dinners, 44
One-Pot Saucy Pastas, 53
Pasta Bakes, 37
Pull-Apart Calzones, 118
Simple Sizzling Salads, 128
Simple Stir-Fry, 47
Melonade, 24
Mexican Pizza Snack, 21

Nachos, 15-Minute, 21
Noodles
    Easy Asian Noodle Dinners, 88
    15-Minute Flash-in-the-Pan Dinners, 124
Nuts, toasting, 13

One-Bowl Baked Goodies, 174
Onion Soup, Hearty, 51
Orange Pork Bake, 61

Paella, Quick, 84
Pantry, 4-5
Parmesan
    Extra-Crispy Parmesan Chicken, 69

Parmesan Bread Sticks, 148
Parmesan Carrots, 136
Pasta
    15-Minute Flash-in-the-Pan Dinners, 124
    Last-Minute Pastas, 54
    One-Pot Saucy Pastas, 53
    Pasta Bakes, 37
Peanut butter
    ice cream sauce, 178 (tip)
    Peanut-Butter-and-Banana Smoothie, 24
    Peanut-Butter-and-Banana Wrap, 27
    Peanut-Butter Fruit Dip, 178
    Peanut-Sesame Stir-Fry, 91
Peas, Pickled Black-Eyed, 78
Pepperoni
    Meal-in-One Dinner Sandwiches, 96
    Mix-and-Match Kids' Pizzas, 111
    Mix-and-Match Potato Dinners, 38
    Pull-Apart Calzones, 118
Peppers, Potato Wedges and, 143
Pineapple Cream Cheese Dip, 178
Pizza
    Mac & Cheese Pizza, 119
    Mexican Pizza Snack, 21
    Mix-and-Match Kids' Pizzas, 111

Pizza Bread, Hot, 101
Popcorn Crunch, 13
Pork
boneless:
    One-Pot Curry-and-Rice Dinners, 92
    Simple Sizzling Salads, 128
chops:
    Chili Bake, 31
    Everyday Easy Rice Dinners, 34
    One-Pan Dinner Bakes, 62
    Orange Pork Bake, 61
    Oven-Tender Barbecue Bakes, 33
ground:
    Island Burger, 106
    One-Pan Tacos, 112
loin:
    Simple Stir-Fry, 47
Potatoes, 48, 143 (tips)
    15-Minute Mashed Sides, 144
    Mix-and-Match Potato Dinners, 38
    Philly Mashed Potatoes, 144 (tip)
    Potato Wedges and Peppers, 143
    Tex-Mex Salsa Spuds, 143
    Zesty Potato Soup, 48
Puddings
    Mix-It-Up Puddings, 165
    Pudding in a Cloud, 169

Quesadillas, 22
Quick Vegetable Dips, 14

Ratatouille, Easy Fall, 123
Rice
    Cajun Dirty Rice, 75
    Everyday Easy Rice Dinners, 34
    15-Minute Flash-in-the-Pan Dinners,
        124
    Great Takes on Minute Rice, 152
    Mix-and-Match Dinner Parcels, 115
    One-Pan Tacos, 112
    One-Pot Curry-and-Rice Dinners,
        92
    One-Pot Rice Dinners, 44
    pilaf, 61 (tip)
    Quick Jambalaya, 75
    Quick Paella, 84
Rocky Road Cups, 170

Salads
    Chicken Taco Ranch Salad, 131
    Chopped BLT Salad, 154
    Classic Torn Greek Salad, 154
    Heads-Up Ranch Salad, 158
    Main-Dish Fruit-and-Cheese Salads,
        127
    Shredded Tostada Salad, 154

Simple Sizzling Salads, 128
So Many Coleslaws, 157
Tangy Broccoli Salad, 158
Salami
    Warm Handheld Sandwiches, 95
Salsa Cheese Dip, 17
Sandwiches
    Cheese-and-Apple on Raisin Bread,
        100
    Club on a Bun, 101
    Easy Dinner Melts, 102
    Grilled Cheese-and-Ham Monte
        Cristo, 100
    Grilled Cheese-and-Vegetable Pita,
        100
    Hot-and-Cheesy Pull-Aparts, 105
    Hot Pizza Bread, 101
    Last-Minute Monster Meatball
        Sandwich, 58
    Meal-in-One Dinner Sandwiches,
        96
    10 Ways with Grilled Cheese, 99
    Warm Handheld Sandwiches, 95
Sausage, Italian
    Oven-Tender Barbecue Bakes, 33
    Pasta Bakes, 37
    Quick Paella, 84
    Sausage Kebabs on a Bun, 109

Shakes and Smoothies, 24
Shrimp, 91 (tip)
    Peanut-Sesame Stir-Fry, 91
Snacks and starters. See also Dips
    Cheese-and-Cracker Partners, 23
    15-Minute Nachos, 21
    Mexican Pizza Snack, 21
    No-Bake Munch Mix, 13
    Popcorn Crunch, 13
    Quesadillas, 22
    Shakes and Smoothies, 24
    Snacktivities for Kids, 27
    Tex Mix, 13
    Vegetable Partners, 18-19
Soups
    Cheesy Broccoli Soup, 50
    Cheesy Minestrone Soup, 51
    Hearty Onion Soup, 51
    Tex-Mex Corn Chowder, 51
    Zesty Potato Soup, 48
Spaghetti Squash Parmigiana Bake,
    120
Spinach
    Cheese-and-Spinach Casserole, 120
    Spinach Dip, 14
Stir-fries
    Peanut-Sesame Stir-Fry, 91
    Stalk-of-the-Town Stir-Fry, 139

Simple Stir-Fry, 47
Stuffings Simplified, 153
Sweet potatoes, 79 (tip)
    15-Minute Mashed Sides, 144
    Praline Sweet Potatoes, 79

Tacos
    Double-Decker Tacos, 80
    Muchos Tacos Master Mixture, 80
    Noodle Taco Bowls, 80
    One-Pan Tacos, 112
    Taco Burger, 106
Tex-Mex Corn Chowder, 51
Tex-Mex Salsa Spuds, 143
Tex Mix, 13
Tomatoes, 135 (tip)
    Green Beans and Tomatoes
      Italiano, 140
    Tomato Cheese Bread, 149
    Tomatoes and Zucchini au Gratin,
      135
Tortillas
    Double-Decker Tacos, 80
    15-Minute Fajitas, 116
    Mexican Pizza Snack, 21
    Noodle Taco Bowls, 80
    Peanut-Butter-and-Banana Wrap, 27
    Taco Burger, 106

tortilla cups, 80 (tip)
Tropical Delight, 170
Tuna
    Everyday Easy Macaroni Dinners, 57
    One-Pot Rice Dinners, 44
Turkey
breast:
    One-Pan Dinner Bakes, 62
cooked:
    Club on a Bun, 101
    Easy Dinner Melts, 102
    Hot-and-Cheesy Pull-Aparts, 105
    Meal-in-One Dinner Sandwiches,
      96
    Quesadillas, 22
cutlets:
    Everyday Easy Rice Dinners, 34
ground:
    One-Pan Tacos, 112
Turnip
    15-Minute Mashed Sides, 144

Veal
    Everyday Easy Rice Dinners, 34
Vegetable Dips, Quick, 14
Vegetable Kebabs, Cheese-and-, 27
Vegetable Partners, 18
Vegetable Pie, Sky-High, 122

Vegetable sides, 5 (tip)
    Cheese-and-Garlic Green Beans,
      140
    Creamy Cauliflower Medley, 135
    15-Minute Mashed Sides, 144
    Glazed Carrots, 136
    Green Beans and Tomatoes
      Italiano, 140
    Miracle Broccoli Bake, 139
    Parmesan Carrots, 136
    Pickled Black-Eyed Peas, 78
    Potato Wedges and Peppers, 143
    Praline Sweet Potatoes, 79
    Seasoned Collard Greens, 76
    Sky-High Vegetable Pie, 122
    Stalk-of-the-Town Stir-Fry, 139
    Tex-Mex Salsa Spuds, 143
    Tomatoes and Zucchini au Gratin,
      135
    Tricolor Green Bean Salute, 140
    Zucchini and Carrots, 136

Zucchini, 19, 123 (tips)
    Easy Fall Ratatouille, 123
    Tomato and Zucchini au Gratin,
      135
    Zucchini and Carrots, 136
    Zucchini Puffs, 123

NOTES

NOTES

NOTES